CW01498969

1

HE OPENS THE trap door and I know that I have to step inside. I don't say anything – I can't utter a word when it is just the two of us. I descend the steep stairs that lead down to the coal cellar, praying silently. It is dark and it smells of mildew. The trap door slams shut. What happens next is what I have spent half my life trying to forget. There is no picture of the Virgin Mother in the cold cellar, cradling the Baby Jesus, as there is in the house. Downstairs, in Grandpa's bedroom it hangs in a black frame above his futon and I like to look at the picture on the wall, feeling the peace. I sense that even though the world can be cruel, there is always beauty in heaven.

Stories heal the soul. There's relief in giving the wings of fiction to life's secrets and watch them trailing up to heaven like an offering of incense.

"It does no good," my mother said on her deathbed, "carrying your past around on your back. Write your story; the good and the bad." She looked right into the eyes of her sixty-one-year-old child, a child who yearned to reveal her untold story. When she encouraged me to write she asked me not to spare her in my reckoning.

A few days later she passed on. I keep her old letters and photographs at my house. Every now and then I sit on my red velvet sofa, the one my mother kept aside for me, flick through photos of people long gone and read crumpled letters. That's how I manage to move closer to my people, closer to my past. Tonight, I will wrap my mother's dark pink shawl around me (the one she crocheted as a gift for my fifty-fifth birthday), turn the radiator up against the bitter cold of Reykjavik's winter night and review my personal story.

The memories stretch far back, but I must have forgotten so many things. I've never been particularly good with dates or with remembering facts or names, but I do recall how I felt in whatever crucial situation I found myself – and how I coped. Not everything that has happened to me belongs in a book. Real people are frequently unbelievable characters, and in an account like this it's imperative to choose well and leave certain things out.

The ghost that arose out of my childhood silence forces its way on to the stage. It demands to take over the space and be the main character in my book. If I allow it to happen, nothing will be said out loud. "You cannot write about the surrounding silence in your life unless you give it a shape," it hisses, while fighting for its existence. Silence has been my worst enemy through my entire life. The silence I carried with me created a chasm between me and the rest of the world. I have to get rid of this ghost so I can finally speak up and write my story.

Somewhere deep inside I have a memory of moments passing as I suckled at my mother's breast. I drank the so-sweet milk, stopped to watch it trickle down her chest before I suckled again. I let go and looked at my mother's breast, then at her face, then at her breast again. I played with the nipple and watched the brown aureole grow and shrink. The memory is hazy, but the recollection of the emotion is strong, like my longing to remember all the people that have influenced me, to reminisce about old times and

4

AND THE SWANS BEGAN TO SING

TO SING

Thora Karitas Arnadottir

Dear Jonathan
Thank you so much
for coming
Best of luck
Thora Karitas

Wild Pressed Books

This book is a work of creative non-fiction based on a true events. The publisher has no control over, and is not responsible for, any third party websites or their contents.

And the Swans Began to Sing © 2019 by Thora Karitas Arnadottir.

Translators: Aslaug Torfadottir and Helen Priscilla Matthews
English language editor: Tracey Scott-Townsend
Cover Design by Jane Dixon-Smith

ISBN: 978-1-9164896-0-8
English language edition published by Wild Pressed Books: 2019
Wild Pressed Books, UK Business Reg. No. 09550788
http://www.wildpressedbooks.com

Title of the original Icelandic edition: MÖRK – Saga mömmu
Published by agreement with Forlagid Publishing, www.forlagid.is
© 2015 by Thora Karitas Arnadottir.

To my Mum, Guðbjörg Þórisdóttir.
Thank you for having the courage to
let me write your story.

AND THE SWANS BEGAN
TO SING

arrange my story into a fluid sequence. My name is Guðbjörg Þórisdóttir and I am sixty-three years old when I finally sit down to write my story. I was born on Lady Day or the day of the Annunciation: the twenty-fifth of March in 1952. People used to joke about how I was only conceived because the pharmacy in Husavik had closed by the time my father ran out to buy condoms. Therefore, I could say my existence is due to a pharmacist who went home early, the pharmacist and also translator Helgi Hálfdánarson: known for his great Icelandic translation of the complete works of Shakespeare.

I grew up on the west side of Reykjavik, but my childhood home was demolished in 1985. It was a pale beige corrugated iron house called Mörk, meaning 'limits' or 'boundaries' in Icelandic, on Bræðraborgarstígur 8b. I studied Icelandic at The University of Iceland and have a diploma from the old School of Education. In my studies, I focused on Icelandic literature and wrote my MA thesis on *Vefarinn mikli frá Kasmír* – The Great Weaver from Kashmir – by the Icelandic Nobel prize winner Halldór Laxness. But for most of my life I've worked as a teacher and school principal.

I have always loved literature and have had the privilege of reading fiction aloud on Icelandic radio, Channel 1. When I've shared books with radio listeners I've aimed for stories that resonate with my own experience, books that have given me strength and helped me to heal, in the hope that listening to the stories will also help others.

Lately, with my eyesight worsening due to a rare disease called Benson syndrome, I have started listening to audiobooks. My reduced sight is also a reason why I've had to go on leave from my job as Principal of Breiðagerðisskóli Primary School, where I've worked for almost twenty years. I have two grown children now, who, with their partners, have brought me three step-grandchildren and three grandchildren of my own. I have always been surrounded by children, what with my school, my own children and now my grandchildren.

I've always dreamt of writing fiction and although I wrote a few unpublished stories for children forty years ago I didn't dare to take it any further. I think I was afraid that I would reveal myself somehow by writing, that by reading my stories, people would realize I had a dark secret. I was afraid of being judged if people knew what I had been through. Shame is a cruel and sneaky emotion, I can see it clearly now and I am ready to return it to where it belongs by writing my story. Even though my heart thumps loudly in my chest with each word that reveals my past I know I have to go on, otherwise evil will prevail.

2

THE WATER BUBBLES in the kettle. I put on my glasses and
make myself some coffee. I have homemade cookies in the
fridge; my mother's recipe. They are my favourite evening
snack. I've surrounded myself not only with my share of my
mother's estate, but also with things that belonged to my
father and his siblings. I have acquired quite a few pictures,
of various sorts. My uncle Jonni had several framed pencil
drawings that he drew from photographs of women he found
beautiful. I also have an incredibly large pencil sketch of my
paternal grandpa, Jón Jónsson of Mörk, given to me when I
was eighteen and already a teacher at Skógar near the
Eyjafjöll Mountains. The primary school's head teacher, Jón
Kristinsson, drew it for me from a photograph when I was
living at his home, after it became clear that my grandpa was
dying. I look at the drawing of a bald, grinning man with big
ears now and wonder what to do with it. I try to imagine
what Grandpa looked like as a child, and what kind of a
childhood he had.

My grandpa was born in a turf house on
Bræðraborgarstígur 8b. His parents, Margrét Magnúsdóttir
and Jón Eiríksson, were blessed with many children; ten
sons and a daughter. My great-grandmother also had a

daughter from a previous marriage but sadly she only lived to be two years old. Margrét and Jón were not well off, but Margrét's brother Ólafur Rósinkranz bought his sister, her husband and their children a turf house so they'd have a roof over their heads. Officially the house was called Nýibær – New Farm – but everyone always referred to it as Mörk. My great-grandparents added a stone house onto the turf house, or more accurately they built a kitchen and a small living room from stone onto the dwelling and called it Litli bær or Little-Farm. There was very little space in the house, but my great grandmother Margrét was a sociable woman and she didn't let lack of space deter her from having guests around. Apparently, she handed her friends cups of coffee through the window when they came over to visit, she put her elbows on the window sill and chatted with them from her tiny living room whilst they sat comfortably outside in the sunshine.

Grandpa and his siblings were all unusually healthy for the time and my great-grandparents were considered lucky. The family slept in the living room and the kitchen because there were no bedrooms in the house. Grandpa and the second oldest brother slept on the kitchen floor, and lay with their darned woollen-socked feet under the stove. I once used a photo of a man sleeping with his feet under a stove for a children's book I published and co-authored. The title of the book was *Krakkar, Krakkar* (Children, Children). It was designed to encourage children to make up their own stories and was full of photos and questions to spark their imagination.

I've always been interested in teaching creative writing and in 1982, whilst I was teaching upcoming Kindergarten teachers, I decided to form a creative writing course for my class. One of my students there, Guðrún Alda Harðardóttir, wrote a popular children's book that was later published. The fact that the course produced a book makes me proud and I admire the story very much. The book is called It Can't be True, and it explores the psychological impact on a child

8

of losing a parent. I've used the book as an aid both as a teacher and as the principle when young students have lost someone close to them. It helped open up conversations and supported them with their grief process.

Little-Farm was one of the oldest stone houses in town. Grandpa and his brothers built a new timber house attached to the little stone house and named the house Mörk, in honour of the original old turf dwelling. That is the house I grew up in. In 1985, when Mörk and the old stone house was being torn down and a big grey apartment building was constructed instead, it was a cultural disaster for Reykjavik in my opinion.

After my grandpa moved into the house he insisted on being called Jón from Mörk – he felt you were judged by your status and belongings and it was intolerable to have such a common name as Jón Jónsson.

His headstone in the old cemetery by Suðurgata reads:

Jón from Mörk
Born 22nd June 1883
Died 27th February 1971

———◦●◦———

On the wall in my front room hangs a faded newspaper clipping in a frame; the obituary of my grandmother, Guðbjörg Guðjónsdóttir. She and Grandpa were married on October 30th, 1920. I am named after her, although she never met me. She died at a young age in the March of 1940, leaving three children. Þórir Már, my father, was her oldest son, next was my aunt Bergdís (Begga), and the youngest was Guðjón, or Jonni, as he was always called.

I wasn't really told very much about my namesake-grandma when I was growing up, and I regret that

I didn't find out more about her whilst I could. Somehow the name provided a link between us, and I felt connected to her shadow-presence in the family. When I turned forty-one my mum gave me Grandma's hymn book. I had turned the same age as she was when she died. I've often wondered who she really was, this woman who gave me her name: my grandma that I never met but seem to instinctively love.

Tonight, I open Grandma's hymn book and find the beautiful, dulled, green ribbon that has been used as a bookmark. On the page I read 'To the Father of the Spirit,' (Faðir andanna) words by Matthias Jochumsson, one of my favourite Icelandic poets. The ribbon is faded, its turquoise colour has bled out onto the page in the years since Grandma died.

Guðbjörg's only daughter, Begga, took great care of her mother's things, and I was honoured when she entrusted them to me at her own death. She knew I was drawn to nostalgia and had rather romantic notions around my grandma's life. Begga once gave me a photo in a gilded frame of my father as a young child in his mother's arms. As a young girl, this photograph reminded me of the black and white print of the Madonna and Child which hung above my grandpa's bed in a big, black frame. I only realized recently that the print is part of a bigger painting; one of Raphael's most famous works, The Sistine Madonna.

I now live in downtown Reykjavik, not far from the church Hallgrímskirkja, where I've lived more or less for the last three decades. In the past few years I've been collecting various old items that otherwise would have been thrown away. In my living room, I keep Grandpa's nightstand and wardrobe, once owned by the mysterious French Baron Charles Gouldrée-Boilleau. There is a street in Reykjavik, Barónsstígur, named after him. Next to the nightstand – which is a long pine cupboard with a marble top (just a little loose and made of the same marble used for my grandma's gravestone) is a bed from my mother's region in the North. It is a hundred years old. Above it hangs an old tapestry that belonged to my maternal grandmother. The picture of Guðbjörg with her son, (my father) in her arms, rests on the nightstand below the drawing of Mary and baby Jesus. All these items are reminders; representations of my people who have passed away. The picture of my grandma with my father is a holy picture to me and precious, as my father only had his mother's love for such a short time in his life. Begga also gave me a simple old flowerpot that had once belonged to my grandmother. She passed the fragile thing over to me as if she was giving me her most valuable possession. I can't explain these hoarding tendencies – both mine and Begga's before me – but I know that the family belongings, Grandpa's possessions, are somehow intertwined with my story. They give physical shape to and are evidence of events that occurred, happenings which refuse to fade completely from my mind.

I often wonder if this particular story would exist at all if the matron of Mörk, Grandma Guðbjörg, hadn't died so young, if the story I am compelled to write would not exist had she lived. So many things would have automatically been different, which is why I want to begin by thoroughly examining the situation in the household just before she died. My father was eighteen years old when his mother died and he could never speak about his loss. He seems to have chosen at an early age never to talk about his beloved mother. Begga, the sole daughter, was the only one of the three siblings who could tell me something about my grandma and about what was going on in the family around the time she passed away.

3

I HAVE BEEN sporadically interviewing members of my family for years, gathering bits of information where I can. I guess it was in the hope that one day I would pin down my story. When Grandmother Guðbjörg would have turned one hundred years old, my family got together to celebrate and I prepared a speech for the occasion. That's when I spoke to Begga at some length about my grandmother and the family life at Mörk in the past. This interview has now proved to be invaluable substance for my writing.

Begga, petite with delicate features, was one of those women who only grew more beautiful with age. She had high cheekbones, fine hair and thin lips. When she was a young child she had lost the sight in her left eye, in a moment of innocent playing. She was outside with her elder brother and other children from the neighbourhood one sunny day, and she'd lain down on the grass in front of the Catholic Church to look up at the summer clouds. Just as she noticed a cloud that resembled a plump, smiling angel, one of her friends called out above her to look at something he held in his fist. It was a long, thick straw, and as she sat up, it went deep into her eye. Grandpa once told me that the day before the

13

accident he had been sitting in the living room when he had a vision. He said to Grandma Guðbjörg:

"There is an eye watching me and I feel like I recognise it."

This kind of talk did not surprise my grandma, as spiritualism was prevalent in Iceland. And the day following the 'vision', my grandmother or Bagga (as she was usually called by the family) rushed her daughter to the doctor because of a straw that would leave a white cloud over her eye for the rest of her life.

The day before her fifteenth birthday Aunt Begga tied a brown scarf over her hair and put on her green coat. She was ready to go to the local shop to buy groceries for her birthday party. As she skipped down the front steps, she noticed a crack running through the old stone house next to Mörk, splitting it in two. This crack in Little-Farm must have appeared overnight, but somehow Begga felt it had always been there. It seemed deep and never-ending. She covered her bad eye as she stared into the crack for a little while.

She realized she had dreamt of this crack the night before, she was sure of it. In the dream, lightning had struck a house, cleaving it in two. She hoped, suddenly fearful, that the dream was the premonition of the physical crack in the house, and not an omen for something deeper.

She skipped down to the shop, still thinking about her mysterious dream and the unwanted intrusion of the crack in Little-Farm. Soon, however, the excitement of her birthday party crowded in again; it had been a long time since anything had been celebrated at Mörk, which was mainly due to her Mother's prolonged illness. At the shop, she bought coffee and sugar, along with eggs and flour for the pancakes she intended to make the next morning. She would serve them with whipped cream and homemade jam made from the blueberries she'd picked at Þingvellir, earlier in the autumn.

The dark-haired store clerk smiled at her and she felt a slight tightness in her stomach. She knew he liked her, but pretended she didn't, ignoring the glint in his brown eyes as she tried to focus on collecting the ingredients she needed. During these years, she was relatively shy, even introverted; her life revolving mainly around books. Her quiet personality provoked the curiosity of the neighbourhood children, who sometimes, in their lack of knowing how to interact with her, would shout things out to her as she walked down the street – more in a manner of piqued interest than antagonism.

"Was there a séance at your house last night?" They sometimes called after her, for Mörk was known to some as 'The House of the Spirits,' because of the fact that séances were occasionally held in the basement.

On her way home from the shop, that day before her birthday, she suddenly remembered a conversation she'd overheard between her mother and her psychic friend in the kitchen at Mörk a while ago.

"Seeing a house in a dream is always a symbol of your soul," said the psychic one, as she washed one of Bagga's delicious waffles down with a gulp of coffee.

Whether it was because of the spirits and the occult experiments conducted by my grandparents, pure fate, or something else entirely, a dark cloud seemed to have descended over the little timber house on the west side. Grandma Bagga had been diagnosed with kidney cancer and was in and out of hospital for years.

When she was at home she was never solitary, as my father and his sister Begga looked after her assiduously when they were not at school, and of course little Jonni was always around. Her doctor was Matthías Einarsson, father of well-known Icelandic painter Louisa Matthíasdóttir. He was a highly regarded surgeon and a very warm and compassionate man. She was not only blessed when it came to her doctor, she was also lucky with her palliative care, for she became good friends with her nurse, a lady called Bjorg (unfortunately I couldn't find out her surname), who looked after her both at the hospital and made lengthy home visits.

Luckily Mörk wasn't far from the hospital, for visiting hours were very limited back then. I know that little Jonni, who was only eight when the cancer peaked, used to sneak out of school to visit his mother, whatever the hour. He would take a short cut from the school by Tjarnargata, with the big tower, and head straight up the hill to Landakot, where the hospital stands.

Grandpa Jón took his wife's illness very badly. He couldn't take any time off to spend with her, since he had to provide for the family. He worked as a foreman for an import company called HBen, based downtown at the harbour area. They mostly imported cement and timber. He worked from a large office in a warehouse on Tryggvagata, close to the boats carrying the company's goods.

Grandpa was devoted to Bagga, and was constantly bringing her beautiful presents; a silver pancake fork or a delicate, small platter found amidst the cargo of the HBen ships. It gave Begga comfort, to see her father come home from work, embrace her mother and tell her simply: "I am so fond of you."

In the evening, when Grandpa was sitting with her mother, Begga would use every minute to work through the chores. Usually she went down to the basement to do the laundry. She'd boil water on the stove, pour it into a basin and scrub the clothes hard on a washboard with soap and water before soaking it again in boiling water. Her mother had taught her how to bleach and air dry light-coloured laundry in a special way to achieve absolute whiteness.

During that summer of 1939, Begga had made a special effort to bleach all the bed linen in the house properly. After soaking and scrubbing everything clean, she laid the laundry out on a dry patch of grass behind the house, instead of rinsing it immediately. She left it out overnight, turned it over the next day, and after two days of this very particular procedure, she rinsed everything out thoroughly. It was a huge undertaking, but it meant that her mother could rest comfortably in snow-white sheets. Begga was quietly proud to have taken on most of the housework during her mother's illness. Even better, she suspected her father was pleased with her as well, although he never mentioned it.

I decide to take a break from my writing, and put on my coat and shoes. I get the laundry basket from the bathroom, and reach for the keys to the laundry room. Whenever I put on a load of washing, or pull a load still warm from the dryer, I think of my foremothers. I have to brave the winter cold to get to the laundry room, but that is nothing compared to the long hours of work they spent, in the same cold, manually doing the laundry in my grandmother's time and back into the past. Whilst the washing machine does my laundry, I find myself thinking of my father, and how quiet his grief was. I can only imagine how hard it was for the children of Mörk, watching the deterioration of their beloved mother. They all seemed to have carried their grief quietly, gently. Whether at home or at the hospital my father wiped his mother's forehead repeatedly with cold cloths and injected her with shots of opium, to ease her suffering.

Once the laundry is done, I sit back down at the kitchen table, with a cup of tea. I enjoy writing about the past and bringing characters to life because it somehow makes me feel reunited with and surrounded by so many of my long-passed family members.

"Begga! Begga!" Her little brother Jonni came running towards her as she made her way home from the store.

"Can I have a pancake now?" He clamoured, and Begga laughed at his eagerness. Jonni was a gentle and easy-going child, and she loved him so much.

"You, my dear brother, will have to wait until tomorrow. You know it's not my birthday until then." But Begga herself could hardly wait to make the birthday pancakes and have her birthday coffee with her family. Bagga had been sent home from the hospital earlier than expected, ostensibly for her daughter's birthday, but the truth was apparent, the hospital could do no more.

Begga put the flour, coffee and sugar away in a high cupboard and went to her room to get out her old confirmation dress. It was purple, with ruffles and made from thick velvet. Unfortunately, it had been ripped on one side but her crafts teacher, who lived in the neighbourhood, had promised to help fix it. With the dress over her arm, Begga hurried outside again and turned right up Stýrimannastígur. At number six, she skipped up the steps of the small red house and knocked jauntily. Inside, whilst the teacher mended the dress, Begga chatted excitedly about her birthday. It was pleasant in the warmth of the timber house and she was relaxed. Suddenly, as if a veil or a cloud was being pulled over her, she felt a chill wash across her. The pleasant atmosphere seemed to curdle and reel about her. Her hands shook and she heard a familiar voice calling her name. She stared at the teacher – but no, the voice was definitely not coming from her.

Abruptly, she muttered an excuse and left. She sensed her mother's death.

Turning towards home, she rushed along Ránargata from Stýrimannastígur, but as she ran west, she began to reconsider. Her head couldn't align itself. She wandered abstractly towards Bræðraborgarstígur, practically walking in circles, unable to face going home. If she went home, what she felt might be irrevocably confirmed.

She thought about the séance that had been held in the living room at Mörk whilst her mother was having her operation in hospital. Lúðvík, a friend of her father's, had led it, and they had only achieved uncertain and confusing contact with the spirit world. Lúðvík was a man who was too fond of spirits of all kinds, but in particular those of the drinkable variety – and he looked it. His teeth were brown, his hair unkempt and his ratty, grey beard addled with bald spots. Little Begga had been asked to attend the séance, as Lúðvík, for some reason, believed she was an exceptionally sensitive young girl, whose presence might strengthen the power of the session. She'd been hesitant entering the living room, anything to do with spirits or 'other dimensions' scared her, but Lúðvík could have been right about her because as soon as she entered the room, they made contact with the spirit world. Lúðvík slumped forward and started speaking in a strange tongue. Grandpa prompted him, asking if Guðbjörg would ever be cured of the raging disease in her body.

"She'll come home," answered Lúðvík.

"But will she be well?" Grandpa asked.

He asked the question repeatedly, and every time the answer was the same.

"She'll come home."

Begga believed she saw a tear run down her father's cheek.

The tingle of excitement she had felt in the house earlier had turned to stone in her stomach when Begga pushed open the door at Mörk and stepped into the hall. Everything had changed. Nurse Björg walked past, carrying a tub of water from the kitchen. That was all the proof Begga needed; you washed the bodies of the dead. Nurse Björg, her eyes wet with tears, asked Begga if she would like to see her mother but the thought of seeing her mother dead, reduced to a body, was unimaginable. Unbearable. She wanted to hold on to the memory of her mother from when she was still alive. The nurse gently took the hand of the now motherless child and pressed it against her cheek.

When I saw how beautiful the sky was this morning, I thought it was a sign that she would get better, Begga thought to herself. But then she remembered the crack in the wall of the old stone house.

My great-grandmother, Margrét Guðmundsdóttir, tenderly administered to her daughter's body. She combed and braided her thick hair as she reminisced about the time the Queen of Denmark herself had once remarked on Grandma Guðbjörg's beautiful hair. She had been on an official visit to St Josef's Hospital at the time. Margret washed her daughter's body with great care and removed all her jewellery. She re-dressed her simply. She put the gold wedding band back into the same jewellery box my grandmother had been given as a confirmation present, long ago, and picked out a silver necklace to put around her neck. She drew a plain white sheet across her daughter's still face.

My aunt Begga's birthday was the day of her mother's wake. Everyone shed tears that day. The night before, my great-grandmother had mentioned that she was afraid her daughter's body would fall apart as it was lowered in to the casket, so frail and fragile had she become. They borrowed a church organ and carried it into the house. The priest came, and psalms were sung. After the ceremony, Grandpa Jón and the priest stood on the front steps and smoked cigars.

A few days later, the window frames in the kitchen were removed and the casket was taken out. They carried it down to the Cathedral, where the new priest, Friðrik Hallgrímsson, oversaw the funeral. As the casket was carried out of the church, Begga watched everyone standing so still, the men removing their hats to show respect. After the ceremony, a woman came up to her and introduced herself to Begga as a medium. She said that a spiritual being had been present at the funeral and had been showering the three children with light, to give them strength.

"I was surprised by how much light you needed," the medium said to Begga. She spoke as if it was perfectly normal for spiritual beings to attend funerals along with flesh- and-blood friends and family. Begga said nothing. She felt numb, but during the funeral she had been picturing angels collecting her mother and escorting her to Heaven, just like in a painting of Mary, Mother of God that she had once seen in a Sunday supplement.

Little Jonni, the youngest brother, was only eight when his mother died. He didn't know how he felt, as he walked behind the casket. He knew something terrible had happened, something that meant nothing would ever be the same again, and feared that life would never be as good as it could have been.

A few weeks before the end of term, Jonni had caught head lice at school. Begga had watched her mother try to comb his hair, lifting her arm again and again before finally lapsing into tears. She was too feeble to help her son. That memory, one of so many of his mother, would stay with Jonni for the rest of his life.

During the first few years after their mother's death, Begga was hyper-alert and sensitive to even the slightest general mention of motherhood. She would for example turn off children's programmes on the radio, fearing that hearing the word 'Mummy' would be too hard on Jonni. When Guðbjörg was on her deathbed, she had made Begga promise to take care of her youngest brother, to keep him safe and protect him as well as she could. At the time Begga did not have knowledge of her brother's ultra-sensitive nature, a disposition that would later develop into a complicated mental illness, but she kept her promise to her mother. She looked after him for the rest of her life, becoming a kind of surrogate mother for him. By asking Begga to watch out for him, it was as if Guðbjörg had foreseen that her youngest would always be in need of special care, long past childhood.

My grandmother Guðbjörg, that Matron of Mörk, was not talked about very much after her death. The same as everyone else in the family, Begga barely spoke about what had happened, particularly not to her father. But one thing she did tell him was about hearing her mother's voice call out to her when she was at her teacher's house, the afternoon of her mother's death.

"That might not be so strange," he said. "Your name, called out, was your mother's last word."

21

4

GRANDPA JÓN WAS a mountaineer, as was his father who was one of the first Icelanders to work as a mountaineer-guide around the country. He took many visitors out, deep into the rugged and beautiful depths of Iceland. Grandpa Jón was young when he followed in his father's footsteps towards the mountains, finding himself deeply attracted to the space and sense of freedom he found within their heights. He said hiking was the best salve for the soul; a way to forget yourself for a time and refresh your spirit. When he walked in the highlands he felt as close to being in heaven as it was possible to be on earth, it was his solace. After Grandma died, I imagine all he wanted to do was climb to the top of a mountain and from there (in his own words) somehow 'merge into the Heavens.'

In connection with his love of the mountains and wandering high, Grandpa, as a young man, enjoyed working as a shepherd. Even though in his life he became a respected foreman and was made an honorary member of the Foreman Association of Reykjavik, he always missed his old job as a shepherd.

"As a shepherd, you are alone in the mountains with your sheep, your thoughts and God. It is simple and good. It makes you humbly aware of your minor place in the grand scale of

Nature." He said these words in a detailed interview in the local newspaper which came out on the twenty-second of June in 1963. It was an article about my grandpa, looking back on his life on his eightieth birthday.

When my grandma Guðbjórg died, it became very difficult for Grandpa to escape from the city to the mountains. He did not have a housekeeper, and couldn't afford to take time off work because he had three children to provide for on an already meagre wage. His mother Margret had died three years before, in 1937, and the other Margret, his mother-in-law, soon became incapacitated, falling and breaking her thigh-bone shortly after Guðbjórg's death. It left left her bedridden. When this happened the children – Jonni, Begga and my father, Þórir – were sent to live with family at the farm Síðumúlaveggir on Borgarfjörður Bay.

The children stayed there, on and off, for several years and were well cared for. Whilst they were away Grandpa stayed in Reykjavik working, but he wrote long, thoughtful letters to his children; that clearly show his love for them. My father and his siblings helped out on the farm; learning how to cut grass with a scythe and muck out the barns.

There is a poignant letter written by Jonni to his father in the summer of 1941, in which he sends his love to his grandmother Margret and hopes that she will recover from her broken thigh-bone soon. A few weeks later she, too, passed away.

Not long after Grandma Bagga died, my grandpa started seeing her former nurse, Bjorg. When his daughter Begga came back from staying at the farm she was not happy about this development and made it clear to her father that the nurse was not welcome in their home. It was as if the presence of any other woman was an intrusion into the sanctuary of her mother's domain.

My grandpa had always been conscious of how deep and far his mind could roam, the depths he could fall into if he didn't keep himself in check. "Too much thinking can be dangerous," he used to say. He increasingly turned to alcohol, attempting to drown out the difficult thoughts. He began drinking seriously again after his wife died and he didn't stop until he was an old man. He knew that drinking wasn't the answer, but at that point he couldn't seem to avoid it. It had started when he was a young man, and before he was married he was the kind of drinker who didn't wait until evening to start on a bottle. However when he married Bagga she made it clear she would not tolerate his drinking habit. Since he would do anything for his new wife, he promised to stop drinking, but still he struggled with giving it up completely.

A few years after their wedding, Guðbjörg suggested that together they should visit Einar Kvaran, an author and President of the Icelandic Spiritualists Association. Einar also led the temperance movement in Reykjavik. When they arrived for their appointment, Grandpa apparently just sank into a chair in the corner of the room, with Einar opposite him. He later told Begga that as soon as he entered the house, he felt as if all his energy was being sucked out of his body. He couldn't explain what happened when Einar was reaching out to the spiritual world for him, but from that day until Guðbjörg passed away he didn't drink a drop of alcohol. His marriage and the promise he'd made his new wife gave him a chance to feel at peace with himself, and more balanced than he ever had been before.

When Grandma died so prematurely, my grandpa's peaceful life was abruptly over. One friend who was there for him during this period was the artist Gunnlaugur Blöndal. Gunnlaugur painted a picture representing grief: a beautiful bouquet of roses in a vase, with one rose wilted. The painting hung on the wall in Mörk for decades, and my father inherited it after Grandpa's death. My siblings discussed selling the painting after our parents passed away but we agreed that the painting had played such a big role in our family history that it would be strange to part with it.

Mörk was not the same without Guðbjörg, and the children began to feel somewhat lost. Begga took upon herself the full responsibility for the house and her brothers, and diligently applied herself. She was also an exceptional academic student and my grandpa insisted she use her 'God-given intelligence' and remain at school. She managed to cut down her years at school by taking two years' worth of classes in one year, and was accepted into the Reykjavik Junior College. However, even though she was passionate about books, and her father wanted to make her life easier for her, she refused to allow a housekeeper into Mörk. With some help at home she could have focused on her studies but it was likely that she knew her father's nature and roving eye only too well, and did not trust him to behave with a young woman around the house.

After her mother's death, Begga made coffee for her father every morning. She put it in a bottle she wrapped in a sock to keep warm and Grandpa took it to work with him down at the docks. He would come back to the house at lunchtime, and if he was drunk, he would vociferously berate her whilst she served him. Once he spat his chewing tobacco into the sink where she was washing the plates. She feared her father was possessed by an evil spirit and said a quiet prayer, deciding to trust in the Heavenly Father rather than her earthly one. She often imagined the warmth surrounding her from her mother, in an attempt to fend off the thought that she wasn't worthy of love.

In my opinion Begga became trapped in her own grief. She flatly refused to allow another woman into the house, even though taking care of the house and her brothers was often more than she could manage. Any argument presented to her to allow help was sharply rebuffed, she was beyond persuasion.

An old friend of my grandmother's, Hanna, who was a seamstress in nearby Vesturgata, used to look in on Mörk, and the motherless children. She was married to a seaman who was rarely on shore. One day when she was stopping by, she found Begga throwing some poor woman out of the house.

"The old bastard better not bring another woman in here," Begga said.

On top of the household pressure, Begga was also terribly prone to crippling exam anxiety. She once told me how during her Finals she would at times have to resort to bed, retreating to curl up, feeling as if the whole world was about to collapse. She suffered from a deep fear of not being good enough. She began to suffer regular headaches that reached such severity they induced vomiting. Bright light was unbearable and she would close the curtains to keep the light from hurting her eyes. Darkness brought its own demons though, as haunting images from a faraway world would appear in front of her eyes as if on a movie screen. She told no one about this as she feared she would appear odd and different; this only added to her feelings of separation, putting more pressure on herself.

At school she was ambitious. She worked hard and was well mannered to prove to others that poor people could be proper. When Jonni, who was also a good student, came home from school one day and told her he'd got nine out of ten in a history test, she asked him in all seriousness what went wrong. Her own grades were normally one hundred percent but her perfectionism proved limiting, as her insistence on achieving only the highest grades made it impossible for her to pursue further education. Her anxiety attacks and need to achieve perfection at all times meant that the strain was too much to bear. She would prefer not to partake than achieve anything less than the highest mark.

Grandpa's drinking steadily worsened. My father, Þórir, didn't like his father's drinking any more than his siblings did. His way of coping with it was by keeping away from home more and more, working in the mountains putting in fence poles, as his father had done as a young man. He also looked after a herd of reindeer for a while, owned by Dr Matthias,

27

who had been my grandmother's doctor. The animals were a fine herd, transported from the East Fjords to Þingvellir.

Against all rationality, every time Grandpa drank, Begga hoped it would be the very last time. She became very adept at covering up how he was behaving to the outside world. Shortly after their mother's funeral, Jonni asked his sister if their father was drunk.

"Bússi at school said he was," Jonni probed.

"Nonsense," was Begga's answer. "He just hasn't been feeling well."

Mörk was certainly a changed place after grandma Guðbjörg died. The deterioration of well-being within the whole family was profound and progressive, and only began to turn itself around when my father himself found love. This had a huge impact on Begga, who joyously embraced having a new sister-in-law. Just before she died, Begga told me that she'd never met anyone who had as much peace and beauty to offer as my mother did.

5

WHEN I WAS a child, my grandpa went outside every morning to feed the birds. He stood on the steps in front of the house where he'd tilt his head and put one arm on the stone balustrade, with his palm facing up. He would stay like this, poised, waiting for the pigeons to come and feed. By this time, there were twelve of us living at Mörk; Grandpa, his three children, and their gradually extending families. The children would sit in the window to watch Grandpa and the pigeons. My cousin Margrét, Begga's oldest daughter, and I wouldn't miss it for the world. The head pigeon would be the first to approach, then the rest would follow. They'd perch on my grandpa's arm like a tree branch, until every last crumb on his hand was gone. This ceremony would take some time, and preceded his every day walk to work, down to the office at the harbour. He had a dignified, rather regal gait and would always hold his head high. He usually carried a cane and wore a hat, but this elegant demeanour was normally off-set by a bit of tobacco visible in his mouth or in the hairs beneath his nostril. If I passed him unexpectedly in the street, he would bow, stretch out his cane and bid me good day with a flourish of his hat, displaying his bald pate. This always made me laugh. I had an insatiable sweet tooth and my grandpa usually tantalized me with sweets and money. He spoiled me rotten, and used every opportunity to give me a hug and kiss me. I remember being perpetually physically close to him; from a very young age I would lie with him on his bunk. I was only one year old when Grandpa first touched me inappropriately. The reason I know my age is that as a toddler I often wore dresses with stockings or knee-high socks; this made it easy for him to constantly grope my thighs and feel up underneath my skirts. I remember a specific dress I could only have worn at this time. I was three years old when I told my mother that Grandpa kissed me in a 'different way' to anyone else.

"He kisses me with his tongue!" I said and just like that my mother was informed about my grandpa's behaviour. This was during the rainy summer of 1955. Apparently it rained for eighty days straight and the papers made reference to The Great Flood. I can't really remember my mother's reaction to what I said and I think I wasn't really looking for any response. It was simply a statement made by a child who didn't realize what could be read into it. But I do remember clearly that I told her.

About a year later, my mother and I had a wonderful day out together. I wore a homemade white dress, red tights, black patent leather shoes and white socks. To complete the ensemble, my mother had knitted a red, button-up cardigan and my hair was tied up with a white bow. We went to see an old friend of my mother's, Hólmfríður, who had retired and lived in a home for the elderly on the west side. Hólmfríður used to own a shop downtown and was always very generous to me. That day she gave me a hundred Kronur bill, which was a lot of money in those days, especially for a child. She also gave me a golden brooch, which I still have. She said she was giving me the brooch for having the most beautiful eyes in all of the west side. These are kind words that I will never forget.

Years later, in another time, when I was myself a mother,

I took a stroll with my own little five-year-old girl, a little girl named after my mother. We wore matching velvet dresses with puffy sleeves. We had hot chocolate with whipped cream at a café near Austurvöllur Square, where my daughter coloured a picture in her colouring book. My son had gone with my parents to Rauða-Skriða in Aðaldalur valley to visit the farm where my mother had been born. Two days later we took the bus to Akureyri to join them. On the way there I taught my daughter a little song called 'An Icelandic Lullaby for a Harp,' It is a sweet tune, as if from a musical box. On the bus was a drunk man who listened attentively to my daughter's singing and teared up each time she sang; when we got off the bus he gave her a 100 Kronur bill as salary for her performance. These are precious memories.

Rauða-Skriða, my mother's childhood home, is a little less than an hour's drive from Akureyri. Originally it was a farmstead for two households where two brothers who married two sisters lived together. My great-grandpa, Friðfinnur, built the stone house in 1924 and eleven children were born in the house; six on the west side, and five on the east. My mother's birth was referred to as the April Fool, since she was born on the first of April, two weeks premature. It was a long labour, as is often the case with first-borns, but still relatively easy, and there was a reliable midwife on hand. My mother was named Þóra Karítas, but was usually called Kaja. She was named after her cousin who died from polio in infancy.

My mother used to tell me stories of her childhood in the country. Together with her brothers and sisters, she would play outside all day, either by the Moon Creek, or on the bank of the Skjálfandi River. Rauða-Skriða was pretty much self-sustainable as a farm; they got their milk from the cows, their meat from the sheep, and trout from the river. There wasn't a bathroom in the house when my mother was born – no running water or toilet in the old stone house. Instead, an outhouse, once a cow shed, was used as a latrine, and bathing took place in a steel tub full of hot water in the kitchen. In between baths, they washed as best they could with cloths from heated pans on the stove. Soon after my mother's birth however, a bathtub and toilet were installed in the house. They had plenty of running water, albeit cold, and it could be easily heated for the weekly bath.

Country children led an enormously active life when my mother was growing-up; playing outside all day, unless harsh weather restricted them. Clothing was also changing during my mother's childhood. Homemade clothes of her parents' generation were not particularly sturdy against the constant battering of so much physical activity, but gradually advancement of new materials began to affect the lives on the farm. Shoes used to be made of sealskin, but my mother never forgot the day she was given her first pair of rubber boots. She was five years old when her father came back from the general store in Húsavík village with the display pair from the window. She stubbornly tried to stuff her feet into the shoes, but they were too small. In a childlike parody of the step-sisters in Cinderella, she could not admit this, either to herself or to anyone else, insisting that they fit. Eventually the shoes went to her younger sister, but my mother's pride was restored as their father returned to the store in town for a pair that fitted. Soon all the family had a pair of rubber boots, and they made a big difference to the comfort of life in the country.

My mother grew up sheltered and protected by her grandpa Friðfinnur. The name Friðfinnur means 'peaceful man,' and this was certainly true of him. I never felt scared or threatened by my great-grandpa Friðfinnur, like I did by my grandpa in Mörk, who rarely left me in peace. Friðfinnur cared greatly about the community in the region, and reminded me later of Njáll on Bergþórshvolur from the Sagas; people came to him for advice when they had important decisions to make. My great-grandpa Friðfinnur was a warm and kind man, an early example to my mother and her siblings of how to respect and treat others.

Just before her twentieth birthday, my mother moved from her childhood idyll to the town of Akureyri, where she found a job in a shop. Almost a year after her arrival in Akureyri, a young Þórir Már, my father, also found himself in town. He had been working out in the countryside, laying power lines and putting up fences for the Geirfoss Power Station. That day in Akureyri, he happened to pass the shop where my mother was serving and was stopped in his tracks when he saw her, she was so beautiful. After that first sighting, he came up with all sorts of errands and excuses to shop there. First, he bought a comb, even though he had short hair and never used one. On his next visit, the comb was broken, and the look of sympathetic amusement in my mother's eyes was so enchanting, as was the heartening discount he received, that his efforts to return again and again multiplied. After several more visits, he finally plucked up the courage to ask her out. They went to the cinema together, and to a couple of dances; before long they were holding hands through the town, in love. My father could never really believe that this beautiful, smart and kind girl had actually chosen him. He knew full well that he wasn't the only guy in town who made a special effort to visit the shop, just in order to see the shop girl.

My father moved to Reykjavik in early October 1949, and my mother followed in December. My mother had only been to the capital once before, when she was seventeen, with her younger sister Fríða. They agreed that the city, where you could travel around on a bus, was a very exciting and intriguing place.

Grandpa Jón, faced with the youthful and attractive couple moving into Mörk, became, unasked, their moral guardian. He declared they could not live together under his roof unwed, and so there was a low key ceremony shortly afterwards, in January. This was just a few months after my parents had first met. It is not improbable that my mother became pregnant with her first child on her wedding night.

Reykjavik was expanding rapidly, and even though there were still sheep grazing at Kjarvalsstaðir pleasure ground, my mother felt as if she had moved to a big city. She always remembered the first time she walked down Laugavegur, the main shopping Street; she thought the town centre was frightfully cold. She was dressed according to the latest fashion: a thin coat, skirt and a scarf that was tied under the chin, in the style of the young Queen Elizabeth II of England. The temperature was actually just above zero, but my mother had never felt this cold before, since the Þingeyjarsýsla region where she grew up is slightly warmer than Reykjavik.

There were many things that she missed from the countryside, but my mother with her green fingers, created her own natural habitat. She was grateful for the large garden at Mörk and quickly established a cottage garden of vegetables and potatoes, just as her mother-in-law Guðbjórg had done before her. She encouraged wildlife around Mörk as well, spoiling any wild visitors she came across; she fed pâté and bread to the wrens and redpolls in the garden. She had a way of infusing the world around her with life, whether it was with plants, birds, people or children, her presence made everything flower and blossom.

Most importantly, my mother brought love with her to Mörk. Having the companionship of a caring and capable woman made all the difference for Begga. It seemed to allow her to find a missing part of herself as well as lifting a huge burden of responsibility from her shoulders. The two women developed a true friendship and happily helped each other out with anything, and enjoyed each other's presence. My mother taught Begga how to sew, and they made blood pudding and liver pâté together. They even started a women's club with my aunt Fríða and Begga's best friend Auður and had regular meetings where they would come together to sew, enjoy freshly baked cakes and savouries, and chat.

And then, one beautiful morning in May, soon after her twenty-seventh birthday, Begga came face-to-face with her husband-to-be. She met the fair, handsome and wavy-haired Kristján Júlíusson on a trip to Akureyri with a friend of hers. It was love at first sight for Begga and Júlli - which was his nickname.

Back in Reykjavik, a short while later, she saw him again, talking a walk in the west side. They spoke, and she found out he had a good friend in the neighbourhood, close to Mörk. After this, she found herself thinking of him constantly, and she would unwittingly watch out for him, hoping he would walk past her home one day. Begga had even rehearsed in her head what she would say if she happened to bump into him. She was determined to be brave if she did. A few weeks passed before her lucky day arrived when Júlli walked right passed her window. She impulsively called out to him:

"Júlli, would you like to try my pancakes? They are freshly baked!"

Begga had learned to bake various goodies from her mother's recipes, and at that moment, she was very grateful for her mother's baking skills because after this fateful day, when Júlli tasted Begga's pancakes, they were inseparable. It wasn't long afterwards that Begga went downtown to buy a dress and a new lipstick in preparation for their wedding. Júlli moved into Mörk, and the newly-weds settled into the downstairs flat with Grandpa Jón.

As my mother had brought nurturing love to Mörk, Júlli brought political enthusiasm. He was an ardent Socialist, and since Grandpa was a true-blue Conservative, there was plenty of opportunity for impassioned lively debate. Grandpa Jón's commitment to the Independence Party was forged at work, as Hallgrímur Benediktsson, his boss and owner of the company, was the father of Geir Hallgrímsson, who later became the mayor of Reykjavik and then Prime Minister of Iceland. This influenced the political leanings at Grandpa's workplace, where to be a loyal 'company man' went with being conservative. Jón called Júlli a Communist and they rarely agreed on anything to do with politics.

The upstairs apartment at Mörk was the domain of my parents. In late 1950, my eldest brother was born – just nine months after the wedding. He was cherubically blonde and beautiful, and my mother, only twenty-two, was overjoyed with her healthy baby boy. They named him Jón Árni after both his grandpas, but he's always been called Joddi. My mother had felt well during her pregnancy, and worked at Jón Sím's bakery on Bræðraborgarstígur all the way through to her eighth month. This was towards the end of the Depression, and there was a shortage of many commodities in Reykjavik, including nappies. My mother had to queue with food stamps to buy off-cuts of cloth, which she used for the baby. When Joddi was born, Mörk didn't have a washing machine, so she scrubbed the rags on a wash board in a tin tub. Just six months into the baby's life however, my grandpa gave my mother a washing machine with a hand operated tumbler. It revolutionised her daily life. She had never owned such a valuable possession in her life, and its practical help, both in energy and time, was significant. It even came with an electric tub that you could boil the laundry in, saving her the trouble of boiling it all up in a big pot on the stove.

In the downstairs flat, Begga and Júlli also had a little son, Friðrik Olgeir, born shortly after me in 1952. Three years later in 1955 they had their first daughter, Margrét Björg, and then Auður came along in May 1958.

Not to be outdone, the upstairs flat was also populating. My parents, although rich in neither money nor space, were rich in children. In addition to Joddi – born in 1950 and me in 1952, Sverrir showed up in 1953 and our sister Guðný in 1957 so there were altogether six of us in my family, living upstairs at Mörk. My youngest brother Gylfi, my parents' pipsqueak, was born in 1967. He was fifteen years younger than me and a little gem. By the time my mother had him, we had already moved away from Mörk.

6

MY MOTHER HAD always dreamed of having both a son and a daughter and was delighted when she gave birth to a baby girl soon after Joddi. At Mörk, the pram was kept in the storage facilities in the basement, so my mother would have to carry us down two sets of stairs to put us out for our naps. When I was only a few months old, she fell down the wooden steps with me in her arms. She didn't drop me and no one was hurt but nevertheless she was always anxious of the narrow staircase afterwards, and gripped me tightly before descending the steps.

When Mum became pregnant for the third time, she began to feel the pressures of maintaining the growing household. Probably earlier than I otherwise would have done, I went with Joddi to the kindergarten, and my mother asked him to look after me. The kindergarten was on Drafnarstígur, diagonally across from our house and when Mum looked out of the window she could see Joddi in the playground, holding my hand and taking his role as a big brother very seriously.

Once, when I was about four, and was at home sick lying in my upper bunk, Grandpa suddenly showed up with a large white jug edged with blue. It was full of caramels. He smiled and held it out to me. It filled me with joy as this was a serious treasure to a four-year-old but at the same time I had mixed feelings about it. I was flattered, but it also felt strange that I was the only chosen recipient when Grandpa lived in a house with five other grandchildren. My doubts, although strong, didn't prevent me from enjoying the sweet taste of the caramels which I happily shared with my brothers.

The summer of 1957 I remember as an exceptionally good one. I had just turned five years old and played outside constantly. I enjoyed the company of three sisters, Þórdís, Kristín and Kolla who lived with their brother and parents in Little-Farm, which they rented from my Grandpa. Þórdís was one year older than me and she had a bicycle. I envied her so much for the bike, and despite the fact I didn't know how to ride one I repeatedly begged her to allow me to have a go.

One day, not long after she first got it, I was pressing her to be given a turn, when Grandpa appeared in the doorway and motioned with his index finger for me to come over. I automatically obeyed his silent command and headed straight for his bedroom. I was in the midst of learning to read at the time, and remember picking out the white letters on the black label of a green bottle that my grandpa always kept on his shelf: Brennivín, it said or Black Death. I often wondered why Grandpa always kept a bottle with such a name in his room. Sometimes it was full, at other times half-full and when it was empty it would be replaced immediately with a full one.

That particular day, Grandpa groped between my legs and then I went back outside to play with the sisters. I wasn't especially disturbed by the incident – this was my reality. It was already so intertwined with my daily life, I didn't have any idea how wrong Grandpa's behaviour towards me was. I mostly remember this day because shortly after I came back outside, the sisters were called in for lunch.

"Don't go on my bike," I remember Þórdís saying to me. "You're not allowed to, because you're far too small for it."

This, of course, presented me with an irresistible challenge, and I spent every minute on the bike while the sisters were having lunch. Þórdís was right; I wasn't even tall enough to sit on the saddle and step on the pedals at the same time. However, I discovered that if I pushed the pedals whilst standing, I managed to move forward. When the sisters came back from their lunch, I showed off my new technique to Þórdís to prove her wrong. Grandpa was in the background, watching out for any opportunity to get closer to me. His shadow seemed to loom perpetually over me, as the abuse slowly evolved over the years.

Every night at bedtime, my mother would sing to me and my siblings. She had a wonderful voice, deep and tender, and knew an extensive repertoire of hymns, songs and lyrical poems. We often asked her to sing the song about the Sandman, who would show up in the evening to put sand in the eyes of little children to help them go to sleep. Her version was by the poet Jakob Hafstein. I was petrified of the dark, and often lay there, scared of going to sleep. I was afraid bad dreams would come upon me, but I was also scared of staying awake for the whole night. Sometimes when I woke up startled in the darkness, I feared that the Sandman would show up, uninvited. But there was another character my mother often sang about that I didn't fear. I trusted this man and tried to understand his essence as I was told he was not only a man, but also God, not only God, but also the son of God. I was amazed that it was possible to be all of this at the same time. I was very little when my mother taught me the Icelandic psalm 'Jesus, Our best brother!' by Páll Jónsson and singing it gave me a sense of security. When I got really frightened, I would whisper the Lord's Prayer, or hum a psalm into my pillow.

I was always a child for words and stories. One of my favourite poems that my mother would recite was the narrative rhyme, 'How Odd It Was,' by Páll J. Árdal. She knew the whole poem off by heart, but I loved looking at the book as well, so beautifully illustrated by Halldór Pétursson. It began with the words 'Now listen to the tale I'll tell. . . ' and

41

I would be gone, lost in the story of the young girl given a red dress by her grandmother. In the story, she goes outside to play in the sunshine and stumbles upon a young couple kissing. I recently looked up what year this book was published, and was surprised to learn that it was 1955. I know we got it the year it first came out – so I must have been just 3 years old. Due to my secret, the secret held within the walls of Mörk, I felt shocked about the book and felt it was a 'dirty' one. That's how much I read in between the lines about the kiss that the young girl in the red dress witnessed but wasn't allowed to talk about.

I went through a period of having a recurring nightmare. I was walking down the right-hand side of Laugavegur High Street, one foot on the pavement and the other in the gutter. I had difficulty moving and felt that I was being followed by a strange man. I'd wake up terrified, and it would take me a long time to find the courage to get through the dark bedroom, the even darker hallway and into my parents' bed. My grandpa's snores could be heard loudly on the landing, coming from Begga and Júlli's apartment all the way below on the ground floor. With my courage finally mustered, I would scamper as fast as I could through the hallway to the safety of my parents. I would somehow sneak beneath the duvet beside my father, who didn't seem to even notice I was there, despite the incredibly narrow width of the bed. I've never understood how my parents could fit in that bed. Our flat, the upstairs apartment at Mörk, consisted of Mum's kitchen, two bedrooms and a living room. I had felt safer when Jonni was still living at home, and my parents, myself and siblings slept in one bedroom and Jonni had the other room to himself.

Mum's kitchen was on the left-hand side when you came up the wooden stairs from the lower hall, and it was always a lively room, especially when her friends were over. She had an energetic, loving group of friends, who were always involved in some project or other. They pitched in to buy a sewing machine and they all took turns using it. When my mother had the machine, a flurry of jumpers, hats, dresses and vests would descend upon us in an avalanche of material. The kitchen was by turns a sewing parlour and a bakery. My mother baked cookies all year round, and when I was seven I was honoured with the job of taking them to the Birgis-shop on Ránargata. Mum sold her cookies to extend the family's coffers a little bit, as my father's salary as a labourer was often not enough.

I loved listening to my mother and her friends' conversations – especially about baking. Before Christmas there were passionate discussions over which types of biscuits to make, even though the most traditional type were invariably agreed upon in the end.

Christmas also brought a special smell to the house, as that was the only time of the year that we would buy apples. The sweet taste of the very juicy red Christmas apples makes me feel nostalgic. They put us in the festive mood just as surely as the big Christmas crate that came every year from our grandmother in the country. The crate was full of parcels; soft parcels of mittens and socks knitted by Grandma Guðný, and lamb that she had smoked herself, in the smokehouse at Rauða-Skriða. On Christmas Eve, we would all dance around the Christmas tree on the ground floor at Mörk, and Grandpa Jón would give us bags full of sweets.

Life at Mörk was often good – at least it was up on the second floor, where I lived safely with my parents and siblings. My mother would hum a tune whilst she cooked.

On the south side of the house, there was shelter from the wind, and on sunny days all the children who lived at Mörk would lie there in the sun, with my mother and Aunt Begga. We would lay a blanket out on the grass, and sit and play cards. Or else simply lie there, looking up into the clear blue sky. The Rock was on that side of the house – a large boulder partly submerged into the ground – and we would chase around it. When Mum sat on the Rock she would tell

43

us old stories about the elves, or magical adventures.

But alongside the memories of the sunshine on the south side of the house, and the warmth of my mother's kitchen, there lies a dark shape of the shadow-side of my life at Mörk. The sun seemed to shine on the heavenly staircase leading upstairs where I lived with my loving parents and siblings but all fell into darkness when I descended the narrow wooden steps that led down to the cold basement. What I didn't understand as a child was that it wasn't normal to grow up in two separate worlds and experience both heaven and hell in rotation – in the same house – through all of my childhood.

7

THERE IS ONE particular memory from my early childhood that as an adult I specifically struggle with. It caused a shifting, semi-submerged rift between my mother and myself. It is a memory of a certain day when my grandpa called for me and asked me to come into his room on the ground floor. This was not unusual, he often did, and I went. I was about five years old and wearing a little dress and ankle socks. As soon as I was inside the room with the door closed behind me, he pulled down my underwear and touched me between my legs. Again, this was not unusual. However, at this point my mother, who had been out in town on a shopping trip with Begga, happened to come home earlier than expected. She found me with my panties around my ankles in my grandpa's bedroom. Startled, she lurched inside and hauled me upstairs to her kitchen. I was so small that she had to stand me on a stool, to look me straight in the eye. It was an old red wooden stool with brown feet and no back. When I stood there my mother asked me what Grandpa had been doing with me in his bedroom. I was frozen with fear and wouldn't answer. She repeated the question but I stayed silent.

Getting nowhere, she threw some potatoes into a pot and I remember her forgetting to put a lid on it. While she moved jumpily about the kitchen she kept on trying to find a way to make me say something. I believe that was the moment when the ghost first came into existence. It rose with the steam from the potatoes, solidifying into a thick spirit that filled the room. The spirit was my grandpa's shadow. It scared me rigid.

My mother's eyes upon me were sad and her voice quivered, but I felt frozen in time. I had no idea of how I could even begin to speak about my grandpa, and that desperately secret part of my life at Mörk. Silently, the ghost swamped me with its threat of overwhelming evil, forcing me to submit to the inarticulate fear it wielded around itself. I stayed silent.

I couldn't utter a word even though there was a part of me that desperately wanted to describe everything that had happened between me and Grandpa; I knew my mother wanted me to speak up, but I also knew I had to remain silent. I felt I had to wait endlessly for the opportunity to jump down from that stool and get out of the situation. My mother's desperate questioning had made me realise that I had done something terribly wrong.

My mother didn't want to give up easily so she even tried bribing me. She told me I could go and buy popcorn from the little shed behind Hjörtur's shop on Bræðraborgarstígur, as soon as I had told her what had happened. In spite of my sweet tooth and my penniless mother's surprising offer, I still refused to speak. I just stood there on the stool, as still as a statue, listening to the vituperation of the ghost; my grandpa's strict warnings echoing inside me. After a while, I came to the immovable conclusion that I couldn't say anything, even if I had been promised some sweets as a reward. It not only felt like it would be a gargantuan betrayal of Grandpa, I was also just plain petrified.

A large contributing factor towards why I didn't speak, was that Grandpa had prepared me for exactly this situation. He told me that I couldn't tell anyone about our meetings and 'what happened between us' when we were alone, as the consequences would be horrendous for my whole family. He explained to me that if I told anyone our secret he would be sent to prison, which would mean my family would be homeless, since he owned the house. I didn't really understand what prison was, but it had to be some kind of a horrible place. If I spoke out, the results would be calamitous. I was an obedient child and didn't want to cause any problems, especially such dire ones. After all, this was the man who gave me a jug full of caramels when I was ill and owned the house my family lived in.

Therefore, I kept my vow of silence whilst standing on the kitchen stool; my stomach clenched and hurt, until my exhausted mother gave up. She must have sensed the weight of my silence because despite me disobeying her she gave me 5 Kronur to go and buy some popcorn. I felt guilty accepting the money as I hadn't told her anything. Nevertheless, I went and bought a bag of popcorn and a colourful hard candy. I ate the popcorn and the candy, but I didn't enjoy it as I felt undeserving of a reward. Ever since, I have so often wished that I hadn't kept silent that day. I have asked myself again and again if my mother would have been able to protect me from that point if I had simply told her the truth.

My mother spent quite a lot of time in the basement laundry room. You could reach it through a small door directly from the garden, or by going down the stairs in the front hall. Sometimes when it suited my grandpa I went down there with him. Next to the laundry room were storage rooms, and for a long time he used them as our main hiding place. The storage rooms were actually two decent sized rooms on the northern side of the basement, and I could never understand

47

why they weren't used as bedrooms, since we were severely lacking in space upstairs. The rooms that will always haunt me are the two storage rooms, Grandpa's bedroom and the laundry room which became the fourth hiding place in Mörk. When Grandpa took me down there, he would be very careful it wasn't a laundry day so my mother wouldn't come across us.

However, there came the day when, after Grandpa had already escorted me down to the basement, Mum decided, unexpectedly, that she needed to wash something. We were in one of the storage rooms when we heard her coming down the stairs. Grandpa grabbed me and clamped his right hand over my mouth – I wasn't allowed to move or make a sound. We were both complicit in the desperation for her not to find out and because I too felt the dreadful importance of the secrecy and the horror of discovery, I thought it strange how harshly my grandpa held his hand over my mouth and it hurt. I also remember being physically hurt in the storage rooms when I had to lie on the hard, uncomfortable furniture. Apart from that Grandpa usually went out of his way not to hurt me physically.

Later in life I suffered from acute claustrophobia, which I see now had its roots in these times. One of the worst ordeals for me is, for example, visiting the dentist. To have someone leaning over me and probing in my mouth produces paroxysms of panic in me. I had a molar out only recently, and was eventually given a sedative as I was shaking and repeating *I can't do this*, to my kind and careful dentist.

I also panic in enclosed spaces. Whilst flying I insist on sitting near the front of the plane, in case of a plane crash, and I can't stand lifts. The fear of being trapped appears to be firmly embedded within me.

After the day of the interrogation on the stool, Grandpa was keen to re-ingratiate himself with my mother. He asked me to hand over three books, translations from the psalms by Valdimar Briem, to my mother. They were a gift to prove his

48

kindness. My mother never asked me again about Grandpa's interaction with me. I don't know whether it was a complete denial of what was happening, or if she hoped it had been a one-off occurrence. I guess she could have thought that he wouldn't dare to have another attempt at touching me after almost having been found out. There are so many things I do not understand. I suspect my mother lacked, or refused to allow herself, the capability to imagine what could be going on behind the closed curtains at Mörk. Meanwhile, the violence continued to escalate.

I remember another specific incident, when I was about seven. Grandpa had made me masturbate him in his room. Suddenly he went into the bathroom and directed me to join him. I remember seeing some milky liquid coming out of his penis, and I knew it wasn't wee, but I had no idea what else it could be.

When Þórdís' parents were still renting Little-Farm, there was a coal storage in the basement. The boys in the neighbourhood called it the Black Hole, and said that whoever entered it would never get out again. In their mind, it was a prison or dungeon and sometimes Hell itself. I would watch from the safety of behind the kitchen window when the coal van came and fed the gaping mouth with its black fodder.

Then Þórdís and her family moved out of Little-Farm. The house was empty and Grandpa was the only one with a key. That's when my grandpa invited me into the Black Hole. The set plan was that he would head inside Little-Farm and after a few minutes I would follow.

Two spinster sisters in their thirties lived in the house opposite Little-Farm, and I knew they were regular attendees of church meetings at the Christian Society. I have often wondered if they ever suspected anything, seeing my grandpa go so often in to the house, with me following a few minutes later. One of the women worked for the Child Protection Agency, and above them there lived a priest, who had a clear view over Little-Farm.

The coal truck stopped coming to Little-Farm when Þórdís and her family moved out, for the house no longer needed to be heated. Nobody had any reason to visit Little-Farm except for my grandpa. Horrifically, the house gave him free reign – he could do whatever he pleased, and take as long as he needed.

Since there was a small window at Little-Farm Grandpa took me down to the dark, cold coal cellar. A trap door slammed shut behind us when we had descended the stairs. Even if someone had entered Little-farm while we were down there, they would not have been aware of us.

The coal cellar was a perfect hiding place for an abuser and once we were in there, Grandpa would become calm, almost serene, and act as if he was my lover. It was down in the Black Hole that Grandpa penetrated me for the first time.

8

IT WAS NOT until I was forty-eight years old that I finally went to see a psychiatrist. He lived in a red house clad with corrugated iron on Suðurgata, Reykjavik.   I finally understood somehow, that it was vital I began to trust someone else with my story, in order to move towards recovery. I also knew this person needed to be a man, in the hope that if I dared to speak up to a male, a lot of my fear towards men would heal. My fear of men has always been strong and it was something I desperately wanted to finally rid myself of. With that in mind I challenged myself; finding that there was still some hope in me.

I went about picking my male confidante with care. I had been asking around for several years, and I couldn't wait any longer to make a decision.   When I had finally chosen a psychiatrist, his name and phone number stayed firmly in my notepad for a long time before anything happened.   I simply could not pick up the phone and dial the numbers.

After a week of procrastination and frustrating myself, I ended up sending him a letter, asking if I could come to see him. When he called me in response, and we spoke for the very first time, I was standing in the playground in my school, Breiðagerðisskóli, surrounded by children. He said that he was afraid he wouldn't be able to see me for almost three weeks, as his schedule was so full. I had just started my position as School Principal and told him the delay was no problem – I wasn't feeling desperate and another three weeks would make absolutely no difference. After all my fear of speaking to him, I felt calm when he called. I do remember saying to him, from this early point, that I was really hoping for pure 'talking therapy,' with no medication if it could be avoided.

I was busy with the newness of the job, so the three weeks passed quite quickly. And finally, the bright and sunny Monday morning of the appointment rolled around. I arrived at the iron-clad house, all ready, I believed, to speak up honestly and completely. But once there, I couldn't utter a word. I realised that my ghost had kindly accompanied me to the comfortable sofa in the doctor's nice office. It duly prevented me from saying a word, clamping a firm hand over my face for the first few sessions. Yet I still kept going and found out that the only way for me to make some progress was to push on through the silence. In the end, the doctor and I proved more stubborn than the ghost, and we slowly began to exorcise it.

I realise now that words were not needed to begin with, just the assurance that we could sit together and share this heavy, sad silence that lived in my core.

My doctor had an idea of my story, as I had hinted at what happened in my childhood in the letter I had written to him, asking for that first appointment. Writing it down was the only way I could manage to bring it up. The doctor therefore knew the reason for my being there, and he also knew that patience was necessary in order to develop the trust needed between us.

For a long time, I paid my psychiatrist to sit with me in silence, to listen to my silence, as I stared out of the window for one hour a week. in this kind of psychoanalysis the patient is in control of when to speak and what subject is chosen which is why the doctor had to wait patiently for me to be ready to speak up. One day – when the ghost was still sitting there with me after way too many sessions – it was in the end my doctor who had to break the suffocating silence with a simple question.

"I was wondering, if you would like to see me twice a week?" The question hit me hard in the core of my body. Did he think I was crazy? That was the first thought that came to my mind but I also wondered briefly if he enjoyed sitting there with me, in silence, for hours on end. Quickly however, the ghost beside me understood that this was a countermove, and that soon he was going to be defeated.

"This is going to take a very long time," my doctor explained. Looking back now, I can see how right he was. Whilst enjoying his caring presence and his patience, I carefully travelled through my past at a snail's pace.

Overall, my therapy took just under a decade. For the first seven years I met up with my doctor on Mondays and Fridays and then once per week for the following years. I started off feeling sorry for him, having to sit there and wait for me whilst I plucked up the courage to put into words what my poor soul desperately needed to let out. Sometimes I felt anxious before seeing him because I was afraid I didn't have anything to say. I couldn't find a way to prepare myself before the sessions and often felt uneasy when I sat on his sofa. All the while my subconscious was raging and little by little the words started coming out. A fragment. A moment. A single memory. A smell. A sound. Stairs creaking, a trap door slamming shut. Bringing my dark memories up into the light was a long, slow and challenging process.

My doctor's office at Suðurgata was on the same street as the cemetery where my grandpa is buried. On a bright, sunny Monday, when once again we had been sitting in silence for a seemingly interminable length of time, I spontaneously suggested we should go for a walk to the cemetery. Initially, it was a desperate attempt to avoid a conversation but my doctor agreed to the walk. He probably thought it might result in the opposite, and trigger an outpouring from me. I imagine he hoped that some feelings would surface at the sight of my grandpa's headstone but I knew that I wasn't nearly ready to speak up.

We walked down Suðurgata and into the cemetery, where we found my grandparents' grave. The bones are still down there somewhere, but the flesh is gone, returned into dust. Some in Reykjavik say the coffins move in the ground and they might even have travelled through Suðurgata all the way down to Reykjavík's lake. Nothing happened during our visit to the cemetery. Well, actually, that's not true because something amazing took place just as we were leaving. The swans on the lake, began to sing. I was surprised to hear them from such a long distance. It was a singing so loud they were almost screaming, as if they were expressing what I still couldn't put into words.

———————◦◦◦———————

I am a Toffee-tart, I told the doctor once whilst sitting on his now-familiar sofa. I explained I had come up with the name for myself when I was very young; I was the Toffee-tart. It was rare for the doctor to show any strong emotion, but that time he looked at me hard, and asked me, steadily and quietly, to promise him not to refer to myself in that way ever again. He said that Toffee-tart was a cruel name for a little girl whose innocence had been taken away and her childhood stolen, enforcing guilt where none should be. His words were empowering.

During my decade in treatment, there were many fundamental constructs around blame and guilt that had to be deconstructed and re-explained to me. The child inside me had to understand new concepts, and re-learn some

54

basic tenets of life in order to understand and dare to grow up. It took a long time for me to learn how to speak gently to myself, and feel that I deserved it. I had never been a Toffee-tart!

9

Five cairns are on the ridge,
Midsummer night.
The black sand
And the waterfall.
A blessed sun in a soulful sky
Caresses the ice.
But the fire, Jonas?
Rages.
And a sign post.
Come, tonight, troll of the mountains!
The forest, there –
Cascade
To cleanse me
With your mist –
Try,
Try to melt the ice
There is a golden flame of love,
There is.
It rampages beneath
And you,
A wondrous bright ray –
Can you

Carry and protect
The flower buds
All through this life?

On June 22nd 2004, Grandpa would have been one hundred and twenty-one years old. I had been seeing my psychiatrist for four years, but I was still a long way from being able to talk about my grandpa, and what had happened between us. I did want to mark the day somehow though, and ended up scribbling the poem above, needing to express something, to get some words out of my body. Afterwards, I felt confused with the fiery emotions behind the words, I felt entangled in the feelings without explanation. Strong love and strong hate were intermingled, rampant inside me. Perhaps my poem was an attempt at a conversation between my past and present.

From an early age my grandpa seems to have been surrounded by poets and artists. The writer and naturalist Benedikt Gröndal used to stay at Grandpa's childhood home in Aðalstræti. The older man and esteemed naturalist would take the boy Jón out butterfly hunting on the marsh, where the KR sports club is today. They would also comb the shore for sea cucumbers, anemones and sea shells. The reasons little Jón gave for liking Benedikt were that he was a kind and cheerful man, and as a little boy my grandpa enjoyed his company. He never forgot that Benedikt gave him coffee and bread with a hard, thick crust, which back then was a delicacy. My grandpa loved food when he was young, any food and all food. They said he grew so fast, they could hear his bones creaking all through the west side. He was youthful looking, and in good health throughout his life despite his drinking. When he was a young man, he liked to do manual labour, particularly outside in the fresh air. He worked on the burgeoning network of roads across Iceland with Þórbergur Þórðarson, who later became a well-known author. Together they hiked up Tröllakirkja in the summer of

1911 and helped bridge the Norðurá River by the heath Holtavörðuheiði.

In the newspaper interview published for his eightieth birthday, Grandpa said he always found Þórbergur a peculiar man, "as most writers are". The road workers slept grouped together in tents with grey wooden floors, in groups. He told one story where Þórbergur fell asleep one afternoon inside a tent. He has been busy covering glass with soot in order to dull it. The sun was strong that day and fire was ignited from the glass. Þórbergur woke in time to save the tent and himself, but the incident was indicative of his behaviour and mind-set. Grandpa thought he must have been watching the sun through the darkened glass; it was just like him, he said, to be measuring the distance between the sun and himself on the heath in Iceland – before falling asleep.

Other notable Icelandic artists and poets crossed Grandpa's path; Stefán frá Hvítadal and Einar Benediktsson where amongst them. Grandpa received nine gold coins from Einar Benediktsson as a young boy; the very first gold coins he had earned. In return for the coins, Grandpa had helped Einar to get a message to his love, Valgerður Zöega, who later became his wife. Valgerður's mother had not approved of Einar, as he was known to be a drinker. She was overtly discouraging the burgeoning relationship, which made it tough for Einar to contact Valgerður. My grandpa thought that this disapproval only made Einar's love for Valgerður stronger, making the clandestine relationship more delicious in the eyes of the lovers. Despite his young age, he was eager to assist Einar and looked at the generous reward as a sign of how deeply in love the poet was.

Even though he wasn't an artist himself, my grandpa did seem to possess something akin to an artistic temperament or understanding – or at least he had some tendency to sense things in an original way. In 1907, he was part of a team building a bridge over Hólmsá River, when he had a strange dream. In the dream, he was raising a flag on a flagpole, but however hard he pulled on the rope, he could only raise it halfway up. He thought there must be a knot in the line, and he wrapped it around his arm, pulling hard in an attempt to loosen the knot. Nothing budged. Flags were folded up in such a way that you had to pull on the line for them to unfold, to wave in the wind, but this one remained low and crumpled. The flag in Grandpa's dream was a large Salvation Army flag, and he could only raise it to half-mast. The following morning, he was sent out to collect wood for the fires and by the time he came back the other men were having lunch. As he sat down with his food, his tent mate, Guðmundur Friðlaugsson came over to him

"Do you mind if I say a couple of prayers for myself?" He asked.

Grandpa said that of course he didn't mind, and promised not to interrupt. After he'd finished praying, Guðmundur turned to Grandpa and said:

"Would you send my love to my wife?"

"Why?" Asked Grandpa, before quickly adding that he certainly would. Shortly after that, Guðmundur walked away and my Grandpa went on eating.

Road work was hard at this time and tools were very simple; they just had shovels, mattocks, iron spikes, planks and wheelbarrows. Guðmundur went back to work moving a wheelbarrow full of rocks along a temporary walkway that had been constructed over a waterfall on stone pillars. He'd done this many times before, had spent most of the morning doing this, but this time the wheelbarrow hit the corner of one of the pillars and Guðmundur was tipped into the water. Grandpa heard the shouting and ran over. By the time he realised what was going on, it was too late. Guðmundur had fallen into the middle of the waterfall. He had managed to crawl onto a semi-submerged ridge in the middle of the river but he was concussed, and fell back into the river and drowned. The wheelbarrow remained teetering on the edge of the bridge, a solitary glove on top of it. Grandpa's dream seemed to have been a premonition, as he later found out that Guðmundur had been a member of the Salvation Army in Reykjavik. Grandpa never denied the hint of psychic power that seemed to run in the family but he claimed not to feel any wiser with age when it came to spiritual matters. In his birthday interview, he shied away from the topic and said he would rather not discuss in detail the strange supernatural phenomena he'd witnessed in his life.

There were a lot of things that he had difficulty in explaining. He could not comprehend how he was drained of energy that day at Einar Kvaran's house, during the visit that resulted in him not touching a drop of alcohol for twenty years. Nor could he begin to come to terms with the strange images he saw on the walls of Mörk, every now an d then, flickering like on a movie screen. They were pictures of strange animals that he had never seen, that he only knew existed in foreign countries, of foreign cities he had never been to and of strangers he had never met.

His mother, Margrét Magnúsdóttir, had experienced the same kind of phenomena. Once, when she was drying salted fish on the Rock on the south side of Mörk, she saw one of her sons, the fisherman Kristinn Jónsson. He walked up the front steps and disappeared into the house. She was startled as she knew that he was supposed to be out on his boat fishing. When she rushed into the house, her son was nowhere to be found. Shortly afterwards however, Margret received the news that Kristinn had died that very day. He had drowned near the east coast and it was understood that he had been drunk when he fell overboard.

Grandpa also claimed he had witnessed a supernatural happening himself. He was attending a funeral in the north of the country, and throughout the funeral he was aware of a woman he didn't know staring at him across the church. When he enquired afterwards who she was, he was told no-one had been sitting in the place he was asking about, although from his description she sounded like the deceased

61

man's wife. The wife hadn't made it to the ceremony though, due to the terrible weather. The woman Grandpa had seen had not been physically present.

In his eightieth birthday interview, Grandpa said he felt no more knowledgeable on spiritual matters than he had done as a young man. He said, that even though he had turned eighty years old, he still felt as if he was the same little boy inside. His outer appearance seemed to have sympathy with his inner life as his hair never aged, never turned white, for he lost it in early middle age. As he got older and balder he resembled an overgrown baby.

10

I HARDLY EVER cried when I was a child, however I remember
one summer night when I uncharacteristically lost control,
and my emotions burst out frighteningly. I was about six, and
it was just after one of my good friends, Áslaug Tryggvadóttir,
had moved out of the house next door to Mörk, and far away
to the town of Kópavogur. My parents were going to make
the drive south to Kópavogur, to visit her parents, and I really
wanted to go as well. When I was told I could not, I burst into
tears, quickly escalating to distraught hysteria. My reaction
came as a surprise to my mother – it was like a dam had
burst. I think my reaction was so extreme because I needed
her protection from Grandpa. This time around the thought
of being left alone in the house with him filled me with fear.
My mother of course didn't know any of this, and thought I
was just disproportionately upset about not seeing my friend.
I was used to my mother being at home and dreaded each
time she left the house.

Luckily, my mother was a stay at home mom, so I had her
consistent presence through most of my childhood. My
father, however, worked in town and therefore I saw much
less of him. He worked for the Post Office, at a desk or
sometimes collecting packages from the docks and delivering

them around the area. He was normally already at work by the time I woke up in the morning, and I was in bed by the time he got home at night, so he was much less of a physical presence for me than my mother. On his few days off, he tended to be exhausted, and napped on the sofa in the sitting room.

The summer when I was six, I found myself without any pocket money left to buy my dad a birthday present – and was feeling sad about it. My cousin, Völundur Heiðreksson, a teenager at the time, had said he would allow me to go with him to the amusement park in Vatnsmýri. It was one of my father's few days off, and once again he was asleep on the sofa. Feeling for my predicament, my cousin gave me fifty Kronur to spend there, but when we arrived, the Kronur flew out of my hands like small birds – and not in the direction of a birthday present for my father. When I had only twenty Kronur left and hadn't even bought any sweets let alone a present, I decided to play one of the games amongst the stalls to see if I could salvage myself from penury. I chose one where you had to throw three balls into a vase, and if you achieved it, the vase was yours. Amazingly, I managed three good throws, and won the pretty flower vase for my father. When I got home, my father was still asleep on the sofa. I tried to wake him, but he stubbornly resisted and mumbled something about leaving him alone. I remember feeling hurt that after all the excitement, I couldn't give him the hard-won present.

Later that evening, my Dad came to pick me up from the playground and walked me home.

"Was I being mean to you when I was half-asleep?" he asked. I didn't reply, but stared at my feet. I remember him taking this seriously, and apologizing sincerely. It was an important moment in my relationship with my father, and I walked happily home telling him about the vase. He was proud of me for winning it. That same evening he spoilt me and made up a story for me about a father who was never tired and could spend all his time at home with his children because he had plenty of money and didn't have to work.

My father loved to ski, and I have good memories of the day trips we took to Mt. Skálafell or Jósepsdalur Valley, where he taught us children to ski. He also taught us to swim, and I remember him tossing my three-year-old self up in the air in the Sundhöll Reykjavíkur swimming pool, making me howl with laughter.

When my brother Joddi was six, he was allowed to go to pre-school. I was four, and too young. I felt this was terribly unfair, and was very jealous of the fact that my brother was allowed to go every day to a place where he would be taught how to read. I watched with increasing envy when Mum bought him a new school bag and fully equipped pencil case, whilst I got nothing. On his first day of school at Ránargata 12, I was lying in my bunk bed, ill. I glowered at him as he got dressed in the new school clothes Mum had sewed for him. As soon as they were out of the door, I was struck by the urge to follo. Not caring about my mother's strict instructions to stay in bed. I put my rain boots over my red tights and followed them up the street. When she turned at a corner and saw me behind them, she was furious. Shouting at me, she pulled me back to the house. She was furious at my mindlessness in leaving the house half-dressed and ill.

A few days later she found me sitting on a swing in the playground, looking surly. Slowly she managed to coax from me the reason I was still peeved. I told her I was upset because I wasn't allowed to go to school like Joddi. Understanding the gravity of my feelings, she came up with the idea that I could found my own school at my aunt Fríða's house on Drafnarstígur. I loved the idea and we immediately put it into action. I duly named my newly-founded school, Aunt Fríða's School and in my opinion, it was a real school that I was proud to attend. I went there every morning for a whole winter.

At Aunt Fríða's School, I quickly learned to read, but when Joddi started talking about break time at his pre-school, I discovered that an important and enjoyable part of a school was playing with other children and eating lunch together. To address this shortcoming at Aunt Fríða's, I asked a friend who lived on Drafnarstígur to join the school. Once there were two of us, I could finally have proper break times.

Later as a Principal in a primary school, I always found that the first day of the school year brought the same tingle in my stomach that I felt all those years ago when I was four years old and walking up the small street, Drafnarstígur, to attend classes at Aunt Fríða's School.

11

MOST OF THE streets in my old neighbourhood are named after the sea in some way; Ránargata, Ægisgata, Öldugata, Bárugata and Stýrimannastígur. Stýrimannastígur is the street that leads up to my old school on the west side, Vesturbæjarskóli. All the rich seamen lived along there, and the street hasn't changed very much since I was a child. The children of the neighbourhood used to race their sledges down Stýrimannastígur in the winter. There was very little traffic so we could slide all the way down to the Vesturgata unimpeded.

I was feeling pretty grown-up when I showed up for my first day at proper school. I was seven years old, carrying a backpack that was almost as big as me, and most importantly to my self-confidence; I could already read. I made friends quickly and easily, and mostly from my own neighbourhood, but was rarely invited to play at the fancy homes of the west side. My best friend was Þórunn Ólafsdóttir, who was not only in my class but lived next door to Mörk as well. I was already a bookworm and devoured every book I could find. One of my favourite writers around this age, was Ragnheiður Jónsdóttir. I read all of her children's books fervently, but the truth was that I was ready for her books intended for older readers, as my experience was so different from the other children around me. I remember being very affected by the character Katla in one of her books. Katla's parents divorced when she was really young, and I took it so much to heart that I asked my mother if I could call the author and ask her to write a sequel where the parents got back together. That's how unbearable the thought of my parents not living together was to me.

Þórunn and I were inseparable. Every morning I would stop by her house, so we could walk to school together. I remember one morning, I sat on the stone steps outside her house on Bræðraborgarstígur 10, reading one of the Katla books as I waited for her to finish her breakfast. I was wearing a beautiful yellow pinafore my mother had just finished making for me, and I was looking forward to school. I remember that underneath the pinafore I wore a white blouse with a lace collar, and matching white ankle socks. I thought I looked pretty good, and I felt good.

I often used the time whilst sitting on Þórunn's front steps waiting for her, to read or do my homework. I loved learning about words – their whole etymology and what they *did*. Some words confused me. I had heard the words 'sin' and 'sinning' from the women who taught Christian theory at the Christian Youth Organization (KFUM). For some reason I loved attending the sermons at the KFUM on a Sunday, in fact I sought out every Christian gathering or group in town from a young age. I loved listening to the voice of the Priest intoning the words, and when this palled, I could always look around at the intricately decorated church or the high dome. The ladies at the KFUM clearly said that the Kingdom of God belonged to the children, but on the topic of sin they were vague. I wondered whether it was possible to be both at the same time, a child and a sinner, or whether sin existed only in the realm of the grown-up. I hoped the latter was the case. There was something fascinating, but deeply uncomfortable, in the songs of these women. I sensed that they were trying to hide the truth by wrapping it up in mysterious phrases

68

like 'Original Sin.' I would think about these cryptic words for hours, trying to decipher their meaning and gain some understanding of life. This curiosity drove me to read everything I possibly could.

On the day of the yellow pinafore, Þórunn and I walked to school as normal, with the accompaniment of the birds singing about the advent of spring. When we got to our classroom, we found that a substitute teacher would be taking the class instead of our regular teacher. The first class was Maths. Just as I sat down in my seat, I realised I needed the toilet, so I raised my hand.

"Please may I go to the toilet?" I asked.

"Of course," came the reply.

I hurried out, and was soon back in my seat, doing my work. However, it was not long until I felt the need to go again. I raised my hand.

"Please may I go to the toilet?" I asked once more.

One of my classmates was sniggering behind me.

"Don't be silly," Guðbjörg," said the substitute teacher, "you just went."

"But I really need to go again," I insisted, politely.

"You can hold it in until break time," came the response.

But I couldn't. I tried so hard to hold it, but eventually it beat me. I stood up and the warm liquid came trickling down my legs in front of the whole class. Of course, I was mortified and ran off to the bathroom to try to clear it up.

When the day finally passed and I got home from school, my mother's friends were at Mörk, visiting. I couldn't even look them in the eye. I was so ashamed; I had wet myself, I had wet myself in my lovely new yellow pinafore that my mother had made so beautifully for me.

What I couldn't know, and didn't realize for many years, was that I had contracted a UTI infection, causing the discomfort and my frequent need to go to the toilet. One physical effect of constantly having my grandpa's dirty hands inside and around my most sensitive area was that I contracted chronic infections. Grandpa rarely had clean hands, his fingernails were generally long and unkempt, with tobacco underneath them. I remember I used to particularly hate it when Grandpa had long fingernails; for it was painful and undoubtedly made me vulnerable to dangerous scratches, and susceptible to infection. Notwithstanding any other damage that was being incurred, simply the effect of the sexual violence on my physical health was obvious.

———◦◦◦———

My grandpa lived in the ground floor flat at Mörk, with Aunt Begga, Júlli and their children right up to his death, at the age of eighty-eight. As he aged, he spent more and more time on his cot in his room, finally only leaving it to go to St Joseph's for his final few weeks on this earth. This was the same hospital where his wife Guðbjórg had stayed during her illness, and from his room Grandpa had similar views over the Christ's Church as Grandma Guðbjórg used to have.

After Guðbjórg's death, all her children had emotional difficulty with St Joseph's. My father had to go there once, as an adult, for appendicitis, and he refused to stay at the hospital for longer than was absolutely necessary for the operation. He even rejected the advice to lie down for immediate rest and checked himself out at the earliest possible moment. The affiliation in his mind between his mother in pain, nearing the end, and the building was too strong. He missed his mother for the rest of his life, and was never able to express his sorrow. I asked him once to tell me something about the period when he lost his mother:

"I nursed her on her deathbed. There is nothing more to say," was his answer and I didn't dare to ask anything further.

There was so much sorrow in the house after my namesake's death and my grandpa sank deeply into it.

"It was awful! There was a terrible fear for the future, about what would happen," Aunt Begga once told me about the time just after her mother's death. She added:

"Grandma was mourning her daughter and Dad was mourning his wife. Poor Jonni, nobody paid any attention to his feelings. We all had enough dealing with our own problems."

Jonni was only eight years old when his mother died. In those years no one talked, or even thought about how a child deals with a parent's loss. He experienced his first psychotic breakdown when he was a young man in college and soon after, he dropped out of school. By then he'd joined Jehovah's Witnesses and was busy going house to house to spread the faith and talk to people. He became a patient at the Kleppur psychiatric hospital. For the first couple of years he was an inpatient, but later he was only there intermittently. He was diagnosed with schizophrenia. My father didn't like the fact that his brother needed to be hospitalised and wondered why this had happened to him. He kept looking for an explanation and thought for a while that the root could be found in the fact that Jonni had hit his head on a hard stone floor as a child. This was the most rational explanation my father could think of. He never even considered that grief caused by their mother's death could have been a factor. He visited his brother in hospital as often as possible and brought him home regularly to Mörk. When I went along with my father to pick him up at Kleppur, I thought it was very strange that I wasn't allowed to visit the mental hospital with him. Curious, I waited in the car and wondered what it was that I wasn't allowed to see.

Whenever Jonni came to visit I'd watch him attentively. He'd pace the corridor upstairs back and forth, fast, like he was pondering something very significant. Every now and then he'd pause, as if unsure of where to go and then he would quickly turn around. I'd be sitting at the top of the stairs observing and wondering why he felt the need to turn around so often and why he'd swing his leg around like that at every turn.

Jonni would regularly cut pictures of beautiful women out of magazines and he collected various newspaper clippings in a box he kept in a small drawer. He also spent a considerable amount of money having huge portraits painted of the photographs of the beautiful women, some of whom were topless. Sometimes he'd go into town late at night and kick cars and lampposts but those nights the police were usually quick to find him and drive him down to Kleppur hospital. Jonni was always kind to me. He wrote poems, studied book bindery at Kleppur and self-published a book of poetry in 1977 at the age of forty-eight.

My grandpa never visited Jonni at Kleppur and never spoke about his illness. I don't know if he found Jonni's condition too difficult to discuss or if he judged him, ashamed of his illness. Perhaps he lacked the courage to face it. The silencing could also have been the product of the times. Grandpa was wrestling his own demons or trying to numb them with alcohol.

"He was like two different people. One man when sober and another when drunk," Begga once told me. Grandpa and nearly all of his brothers battled alcoholism. One of his brothers, Guðmundur Axel, would go on drinking binges. He'd stay sober for nine months then go out and buy two bottles of Brennivín or Black Death, drink both of them and stay in bed for a couple of days, sick as a dog. This however, didn't prevent him from condemning his brother Jón's daytime drinking habits. He felt his brother should stay sober as he had the responsibility of bringing up three children all by himself. He also claimed that his brother Jón had gone mad after losing his wife, Guðbjórg.

When I started opening up to my family about what I'd experienced as a child, I tried finding out whether my grandpa had been abusing any of the other children in or around Mörk as well. My cousin Margrét, who's three years younger than me, was around our grandpa as much as I was growing up. I've asked her repeatedly about this and she has assured me that Grandpa never put his hands on her or kissed her with his tongue. I can't describe the relief I felt when I finally gathered enough courage to ask her, but after recently visiting Guðmundur Axel's daughter, Unnur, who lives in Reykjavík and is in her late eighties, I finally got some new information. Long before I was born, Unnur, her sister Gréta, and other girls in the neighbourhood were certain my grandpa was a sex maniac. Here I am, in my sixties, and I've found out that I'm not the only child Grandpa abused. "My dad always said that his brother went mad after losing his wife so I assumed that his behaviour was part of his madness," Unnur said.

On Bræðraborgarstígur 4 there lived a widow with her children and Unnur told me that she thought that those children had been targeted by Grandpa. He used to offer them chocolates and cigarettes in his office on Tryggvagata, where he had two rooms to himself, one with a desk and the other with a bed. According to Unnur, when Gréta started smoking as a teenager, Guðmundur Axel pulled his daughter aside and told her in no uncertain terms that she was not allowed to visit her uncle Jón in the office, even if he offered her free cigarettes, a huge temptation in Gréta's eyes. She disobeyed her father only once, visiting her uncle in the office when he had promised to give her cigarettes.

"He thought he'd get something from me in return," Gréta later told her sister and added:

"I told him I didn't think so and ran out as fast as I could!" Unnur is also certain her friend Guðlaug, who lived close to Mörk, fell victim to our grandpa when she was a teenager. She got invited to the office and was unlucky enough to accept both chocolates and cigarettes. She didn't tell Unnur what else went on that day, but she thought Guðlaug was never the same after it. Guðlaug once said to her that if her little sister Sigga was ever dumb enough to be fooled by that old

73

man, she would kill her.

"We were so stupid," Unnur said – "Of course we should have told an adult what was going on with Jón."

I wish I could have spoken to someone who had a similar experience with my grandpa as me, but unfortunately I never got to meet Guðlaug as she died suddenly the year she turned forty. She'd invited Unnur over for a birthday party, bought a dress and baked a cake but never got to see the day itself. Unnur also told me that Gréta had never understood why my father chose to live at Mörk with his wife and children while my grandpa was also living there.

"Somehow none of us ever got around to bringing it up with your father." These things were never discussed with the adults", Unnur said, as if she was now shocked at her lack of action.

"The generations never really talked to each other, and the children didn't dare to mention it to their parents, but we spoke about it all the time amongst our group of friends." There might be someone else out there who my grandpa molested, someone I don't know of. I remember a troubled boy who lived on Bræðraborgarstígur who suddenly appeared out of nowhere in our garden with an air rifle. He was there to shoot Grandpa's pigeons, he said. He proceeded to do so. Grandpa was out, but when he returned he was shocked. He said the pigeons would never return, as the boy had managed to kill the lead pigeon, and he was right. Why the boy took this act upon himself is unknown, but the sheer randomness of the event could be seen as suspicious.

As time went on, and my slow process of self-healing progressed, I started gathering information on sexual violence against children generally. It seemed to me that relatively small changes in awareness and care could make a huge difference. I see now how children are taught about the sanctity of their private parts and I think that is a very good thing, as I grew up feeling that my own did not really belong to me. Interestingly, what I have found as I gradually collate information, is that within the diversity of the people who can be classed as paedophiles, they can more or less be divided into two groups; those who actively molest children, and those who don't. It's clear to me that all these people need to have access to help and support in order for children to be safe from them. However, that demands a calm and logical discussion around these matters. I am totally against the silencing of the discussion around sexual violence against children, or it being run on hate. Merciless judgement can lead to more offences.

I wonder whether my grandpa was a dyed-in-the-wool paedophile, or whether he 'just' took advantage of those around him. I suppose it doesn't make any difference, the outcome is the same. In some ways he definitely 'courted' me; not least with his attention and presents of caramels – and he could treat me like a princess. But he would also grab me at every chance he got, satisfying his needs wherever he could manage, whether it was in the coal cellar, or on the hard furniture of the storage room. I believe he *did* know what he was doing – and what the consequences would be upon me – but it didn't stop him. Despite his long-term 'relationship' with me, I have tended to believe he was more of a 'situational rapist' than a paedophile. He just seemed unable to leave women alone, whatever age they were; so his interest was definitely not limited to children.

It's difficult to admit but getting confirmation that I wasn't the only child my grandpa abused was a certain relief. That knowledge has brought answers to many of the difficult questions I've been dealing with my entire life. As a child I often asked myself if my situation with Grandpa had been caused by my name. I've spent countless hours wondering if I in some sense took over my grandma's role as a wife when she died because we have the same name. My childish mind reached the simple conclusion that my fate would have been less cruel if only I'd been named after my other grandma, Guðný, while the real truth is that I was born into the home

75

of a sex maniac who had inappropriate feelings towards his grandchild and let himself indulge them. The new information from cousin Unnur helps when it comes to correcting all these misconceptions. Although I find it hard to get my head around all of this, I know it is important to put the blame and shame back where it belongs, so the child within me can be free from the lies I've lived with my whole life.

12

IN NOVEMBER 1961, when I was nine, my mother fell suddenly and seriously ill. I remember the day exactly; the preparations for Christmas had already begun, and earlier that morning I had gone into town with my parents to pick out new Christmas shoes. We had taken Dad's mail truck and driven to the shoe shop on Hverfisgata. I had picked brown, square-toed little pumps that I thought were terribly mature, and was feeling very pleased with myself. I remember stepping out of the shoe shop and directly onto a patch of damp cement where new paving was being laid. I remember the feeling of guilt that I had spoilt the pristine surface that the workmen had worked so hard to make. Then we all went home. There was boiled haddock for dinner. My father put fish oil on my younger siblings' plates, which Joddi and I thought disgusting – we would have nothing but butter. We all enjoyed our dinner until I suddenly noticed Dad staring at Mum.

"My goodness Kaja," he began. "Your eyes are so yellow."

At this, Mum got up from the table, frowning, to have a look in the mirror. Dad followed her into the bathroom. Our dinner got cold. That afternoon Mum went to see the doctor and was immediately admitted to the hospital. She had severe jaundice.

The next thing we knew, Mum's younger sister Disa had taken the bus down south to see us. She had recently moved from Rauða-Skriða to Akureyri where she worked at the Lindt chocolate factory. From there she sent us sweets, and when she came to Mörk, she brought chocolates, cookies and cream puffs. We loved Disa. She was only eighteen; young, blond and beautiful and when she arrived for this sudden visit, she took over the running of the household from my mother, like a sweet-smelling angel. She cooked our dinners, washed our clothes and generally watched over us when Dad was at work.

Mum remained in the hospital for months. Looking back, I think her absence emboldened my grandpa – it was as if he was less scared of his actions towards me being found out. It was in this period that Grandpa started taking me to the old stone house.

Christmas was different that year. Mum wasn't there to sew my Christmas dress or bake the cookies that we traditionally ate accompanied with generous quantities of creamy milk. Christmas time was a sacred time in my mother's eyes. She took the festivities very seriously and always managed to create a holy atmosphere. She would start the preparations with her annual Christmas cleaning of Mörk, when she would clean the house even more thoroughly than usual, and then the decorating would begin. The Christmas tree would traditionally be decorated on the twenty-third of December (Mass of St. Thorlac) but the great Christmas Star would light up our window from early December. There was a wreath with four candles that would light up the living room and my mother hand-made a special advent calendar with tiny parcels that she bought for all her children to open each day of December until Christmas. She baked a tall gingerbread house and turned on the Christmas Lights. She also hand-made a Christmas tablecloth. Everything she did contributed to the holy atmosphere she created for us.

The Christmas period was very busy for my father at work as a postman. He had to get up terribly early each day and was tired all the time. Despite the fact that he found it difficult to wake up every morning and get out of bed he never showed up late to work thanks to his invention: the two-alarm method. He put two alarm clocks into two separate Quality Street tins and set them to go off twenty minutes apart. He would be sure of waking up by the time the second alarm started. All through December and then until about midday on Christmas Day itself he worked non-stop. As soon as all the Christmas packages had been safely delivered to the citizens of Reykjavik, Dad came home to Mörk and fell asleep.

My grandma Guðný had sent her annual package from the country, full of goodies, and we each got new mittens, woolly socks and smoked lamb. But nothing felt the same that year. Mum had been allowed home from hospital on Christmas Eve. I almost didn't recognise her. She appeared a hollow shell of her former self, especially against the backdrop of her usually favourite time of Christmas. She arrived shortly after we had finished dinner but only managed to stay for an hour before she had to return to the hospital. She was too weak to give anything of herself and it saddened her deeply.

A short while later, Dad's face turned yellow.

It was in February following the Christmas that Mum had become ill. After that, we weren't allowed to visit Mum in the hospital at all, as the doctors thought it must be contagious. After all, Dad had caught it from her. It was decided that all us children would go to stay with family in the north, although Joddi, the eldest, would stay In Reykjavik with Aunt Begga.

Not long before I was due to leave Reykjavik, I was walking home from a PE class with a school friend when I happened to mention to her that both my mother and father had jaundice. At this, she nonchalantly turned to me and said

"That's how Elin lost her mum. She got jaundice and died."

79

I hadn't realised that my mother could die of jaundice until that moment, and shock waves rolled through me as I feared for my mother's life.

Before I went up north, Aunt Begga took me to visit my mother in hospital. She had just had a lumbar puncture and was too weak to even speak to me. There was hardly any life left in her and it left me petrified. I thought about death, and poor Elín who had lost her own mother to jaundice. I wondered if it was possible Death would pay a visit to my mother at the hospital and take her away from me. Then a horrible thought struck me: Could it be possible that my mum and dad would both die from this dangerous disease? This question plagued me all the way to the airport with Aunt Fríða and her husband Stefán, and I decided to consciously steer my thoughts away from this dark area and try to think about something more uplifting.

During this difficult period, myself, my little sister Guðný and our younger brother Sverrir, all flew north with Fríða and Stefán. They had recently moved to Húsavík, where they'd built a house that was thought to be the nicest one in the village. Sverrir then continued his journey even further into the country, to stay with our grandmother Guðný and Uncle Teddi, whilst we remained in the village. Sverrir had been sent to live with Grandma before, to reduce the burden on our mother, so he was relatively comfortable with the set-up. It had been for about a year and a half when he was five. Sverrir used to joke that he was sent back there because he was the naughtiest of the siblings and needed to be kept far away, but of course that's not true. My parents and the family were just trying to maintain some semblance of security for us, with what we knew, and he knew Grandma best.

Sverrir was a lively boy. When he was four years old, he disappeared unnoticed into the attic from where he climbed out of the window and onto a steep roof. I was the first to spot his tiny figure from the garden, and after sounding the alarm, the road beside Mörk became full of concerned neighbours, a veritable crowd staring up at our roof. The reason for his escapade, it was soon reported, was that he wanted to see the pigeons' nest that was apparently up there, full of eggs. He had managed to steal an egg – which he unfortunately broke just before Dad rushed out on to the roof to get him.

The first Christmas after our parents fell ill, when Sverrir stayed with Grandma and Teddi and we were with Fríða and Stefán, I remember Grandpa Jón sent Sverrir twelve individual gifts, just for him. Grandpa had bought and wrapped the presents himself, thinking of the small boy away from his family at Christmas. For as he said, Sverrir was not only away from his parents, but away from his siblings as well.

My mother told me later that after she'd said goodbye to me at the hospital before I travelled up north, she had stared out of the window whilst lying in bed, looking towards Reykjavik airport. Snow had been falling and when she saw my plane, flying overhead, tears streamed down her face. Her doctor noticed her and asked her what the matter was: "Three of my precious children are on that plane," she answered before turning her head towards the wall. It was hard for the whole family, being separated. I, however, did have the secret relief – amidst the upset – of being separated from Grandpa for a while.

I started going to school in Húsavík, where I soon made new friends. My best friends were Jóhanna and Jórunn, who helped a lot in making me feel more at home, but I missed Mum terribly. I also found the schoolwork difficult as everyone seemed so much further ahead of me in most subjects. An extra discomfort of school was that the man who taught PE kept coming in to the girls' changing rooms – ostensibly to turn on the showers. The teacher didn't do anything wrong but it made me very uncomfortable.

When my little sister Guðný caught mumps I tried to take advantage of her illness to escape school and avoid new challenges. I asked her to breathe into my mouth in the hope

I would be allowed to stay at home too. Just when I arrived at Húsavík, the school was participating in a Nordic skiing competition where everyone had to ski-walk for four kilometres. The competition was held in rounds, between the classes. This had resulted in ski-walking becoming rather a craze, and competition in the school was rife. I was not confident with the activity, however, having barely done it before, and was very nervous when I heard that I had to participate, otherwise I would be letting down my new class. My last chance to participate in the competition was coming up when I asked Guðný to breathe into my mouth. I felt exhausted on the morning itself, but as I wasn't ill I went to school and forced myself through the competition. When I finished the walk I realised I had a temperature of 39 degrees. I went straight to bed and my friend Jóhanna was kind enough to bring me over lots of interesting books to read, and I found I rather enjoyed my little sojourn from school. I remember that one of the books was about a girl whose mother was very ill. It was extremely touching, and I revelled in the character's sadness. I found great relief somehow in identifying with the feelings of the little girl and her story, and I read it several times.

As I started to feel better, I discovered a method I could use to prolong my respite from the classroom. I ran the thermometer under the hot tap in the bathroom before showing it to Aunt Fríða. I managed to fake a temperature of 38 degrees for few more days and was delighted with lying in bed reading, whilst being cared for by my lovely Aunt Fríða.

That was the year I turned ten. I remember lots of new things from that year. For my birthday, I remember clearly how Aunt Fríða gave me a grilled cheese sandwich with asparagus for lunch for the first time. I loved it, and still do. That summer Jóhanna and I started working together down at the harbour, stacking fish.

I thought a lot about Mum and Dad down in Reykjavik, and prayed every night for their recovery. I missed them both very much – but what I didn't miss was my grandpa and the coal cellar. However, I don't remember being plagued by bad memories or dark feelings as such – it seems as if even by then I'd learned to bury them deep down in my unconscious and avoid thinking about the Black Hole whilst I was away.

Out parents recovered and we returned to Reykjavik to be reunited as family. From around this period of time I remember one incident clearly. I was wearing moss-green leggings with an elastic that went under each heel, when Grandpa took me down to the cellar. He didn't just rape me once, but repeatedly, and I was filled with rage over the fact that he would allow himself to take an endless amount of time to violate me.

Tonight, after a writing session, I curl up on my sofa, with the remnants of a cup of cocoa and some biscuits next to me, ready to watch a documentary. The film is about the dark side of the Irish Catholic Church, and the abuse in many of their educational institutions. The documentary made me think of a childhood friend who I knew when I was staying with Aunt Fríða, a girl who lived locally but went to a different school to me. All the children in the neighbourhood played openly together, and, as children do, explored many trains of thought with each other, having different conversations than we would have done with the adults around. I was very interested in our bodies, in particular our private parts; and bums and vaginas seem to have been high up in my priority list for discussion. This preoccupation must have been a result of my precocious sexual experience; I had knowledge thrust upon me before I was ready to understand, and I struggled with it.

There were a few other kids who were intrigued by this world, aware of the thrill of the taboo that we didn't understand, but I see now that my friend was unusually interested, in a similar way to how I was. I suspect that she, too, was a survivor of abuse – from the staff at Landakot, her catholic school. It was indeed revealed year0s later, that there had been ingrained patterns of abuse there, particularly from two senior members of staff. The girl I knew died when she was still a young woman and I do not know if my suspicions are correct.

I am so very relieved I wasn't sent to that school. The danger was always around when I came home from school in Reykjavik, if it had also been at a school I attended when staying with my aunt as well, I truly don't know how I would have coped. At Mörk, Grandpa, having retired, was now at home all the time, and although my mother was around, she spent a lot of time upstairs in her kitchen with Begga. I remember how Grandpa would stand at the window, waiting for me to come home from school. When we were together inside his room, I could hear the children playing in the street. I would think about them, or stare at the picture of the Virgin Mary and Child on the wall, imagining myself disappearing into another world, as Grandpa's hands and body covered me.

13

IN SO MANY ways I was a provocative child. When I was twelve I went with some friends to a concert at Club Lido, where the band Tónar was playing. I confidently asked all the band members to sign their names on my arm, drawing attention to myself. This appeared to rather shock some of the girls I was with, who said my behaviour was embarrassingly forward. I was also beginning to look older than I was as well, although it was probably mostly to do with my demeanour. A friend of my mother's had a daughter who was a hairdresser. For my twelfth birthday, she cut my hair and put it up for a little photoshoot. In the picture I look years older than I was. I have seen a copy of our class photograph for that year as well; the other girls still look like children, whilst I look grown up.

Around this time, the parents of a classmate of mine won a lot of money on the national lottery. They bought a big house out in Kópavogur, but before they moved they threw a big party to celebrate, and all their daughters' school friends were invited. It was a costume party. There was incredible food, Tónar played, but what was most striking was that everyone looked so different, wearing their costumes. There was a photograph taken of me at the party – I was dressed as a fortune teller. It is very strange to look at, as although I know I was only twelve, I am clearly a woman and no longer a child. The party lasted until five in the morning, and I remember it as a truly fun night, but it pains me now to see how much I was clearly a sexual being at the time, whilst my classmates were still firmly in their childhoods.

My aunt Disa married a sailor. He was a strong man and had quite a tough-guy image. When I was twelve, he offered to take me on a drive in his car. We drove from Reykjavík towards Heiðmörk nature reserve, and at some point along the way he pulled the car up on the side of the road for a break. He'd brought a packed lunch for us, which he proceeded to spread out on a gingham cloth on the grass. But despite his effort (or maybe because of it) I refused to join him and just sat in the car, frozen. I was so frightened that he was preparing all this in order to make something inappropriate happen between us. I couldn't possibly make myself get out of the car. I might have got it all wrong and although nothing bad had happened, I felt deeply uncomfortable around him afterwards. What I had learned from my grandpa was enough – I didn't trust men and was glad that I stayed sitting in the car, undisturbed, while he ate his lunch alone on the grass.

The incident with Disa's husband seemed to stay with me, prodding at a weakness. I remember I went walking by the sea on the west side one day not long after the drive and I prayed. During my walk I hinted to God that if any man had to die soon, it wouldn't be so bad if it was the man with the gingham blanket. Not long after this, horrifyingly, Disa's husband died in a boating accident. I was traumatised, blaming myself completely and feeling I had killed my aunt's husband through wishing him ill. Soon after he died, at his funeral, we discovered he had made another woman pregnant. This threw a further complication into the mix of my emotions around him. I felt dreadful for Disa and was deeply concerned over her feelings. I went over and over the car ride and the boat accident in my mind.

My mind seemed always to be churning. My thoughts were conflicting and I felt unsure for a long time if I even had the right to be angry with Grandpa. A large part of me felt I deserved exactly what I got. As a small child I remember eating an ice cream cone and thinking – knowing – I was an ugly girl. I asked God if he would consider turning me into a beautiful woman when I grew up.

In my early teens, and out of nowhere, my grandpa apologised to me. By then, my family and I had moved out of Mörk, and I rarely bumped into him. He had stopped drinking again, and I don't know how much of his sudden contrition was related to this, but the abuse had gone on too long for me to care about casual contrition. I was out walking on the west side, more precisely at Ránargata, when he suddenly passed me. He was then an eighty-two-year-old man with a cane. He came straight up to me and mumbled his apology.

"Forgive me."

I remember my throat closed up. I saw the old ghost twist at his side, and any words that tried to form in my head, froze on my tongue.

In the end all I managed to say was "Ok," in a low voice.

The truth is that at the time I barely knew what he was apologising for, as I hadn't even completely comprehended that I was a survivor of a crime: of abuse. Timing and memory is hazy and I am not sure if the abuse had properly stopped at the time of his apology – although I reckon that it had tailed off before I bumped into him at Ránargata. I don't know if it stopped because he'd stopped drinking or if he had simply lost interest in me, now that I was bigger and not a child anymore. Perhaps he was simply frightened I would finally speak out.

When I was thirteen I went on a visit to Rauða-Skriða, along with my friend. For weeks I'd been looking forward to getting out of town, and seeing my other grandpa, Friðfinnur.

87

I had always enjoyed visiting him, and we enjoyed having long and meaningful conversations. By then he was a permanent resident at an elderly home at Húsavík, but the night I arrived in Rauða-Skriða, he died. I was extremely upset that I didn't get there in time to see him. I had always semi-consciously compared my grandpas; finding it strange how one of them could be so warm, wise and flawless whilst the other was somehow kind, cruel and sick at the same time.

My Grandpa Jón was a man who chose to abuse a child, or children. The reasons behind his choice are ones that I will never really know, or hope to understand fully. I believe that forgiveness has the power to free sexual abuse survivors from the past and prevent them from being burdened by their abuse or abusers for the rest of their lives. However, even though I chose to forgive my paedophile grandpa, I don't expect others to forgive their predators nor does it in any way mean that I accept or agree with what Grandpa did to me.

The consequences of sexual abuse are multi-faceted and the shame is complex. A common result of early sexual abuse is that children become aware of their sexuality far too early. I was ashamed of my sexuality, and of my sexual desire. When you've been abused from a young age, your libido is inevitably active sooner than is normal. It's not healthy to have sexual needs when you are child, long before you've developed emotionally and intellectually, let alone fully matured physically, like I did.

Even though I never, ever, sought to be alone with my grandpa, I still blamed myself for his criminal behaviour. I felt responsible for the violence that was done to me. In my lonely, self-accusatory mind I thought I should just have said no if he was doing something I didn't like and then he would have left me alone, and because I didn't I felt what he did was my fault and I shouldn't complain. Of course, I know now how unfair it was of me to expect a child like myself to defend herself against what was happening in the hands of a grown man. I obeyed Grandpa without ever having the means to protest.

I have also now fully accepted and *know* that I didn't deserve to be sexually abused. No one deserves to be robbed of their youth, but for a long time I didn't have that understanding. I felt I must have been born a worse person than others, and that it justified the abuse.

———◦◦———

I first heard the word incest as a teenager. I was absolutely shocked. I froze, and then a whole new, fresh wave of shame washed over me. The shame overpowered any anger I had, and instead of being angry with Grandpa, I was full of self-accusation.

It took me many years to realise that I wasn't complicit in Grandpa's crimes, that I did not aid him in what happened. I am also aware of how lucky I am that I wasn't born thirty years earlier. Just some thirty years before this happened to me, things were viewed very differently. During that period if a child suffered ongoing sexual abuse in Iceland, then it was likely the child would be blamed for it, and often sent away to a secluded children's home. It was even widely believed that children who were survivors of sexual abuse were possessed by evil spirits and had seduced the men who abused them into sexual activity by forces beyond their control.

It is horrendous to think of how these views must have damaged, confused and hurt many abused children in the past; it must have had an awful impact on their emotional healing.

How a community thinks and what message it gives out about child abuse are hugely important to the individual, and really affect the survivors of abuse. In just the last few decades there have been various forays into how to approach this taboo subject as a society. One idea has been an exploration into a more holistic, family approach. Here, the blame for a crime doesn't necessarily fall solely on the perpetrator of the crime, for example the mother could be partly blamed if the step-father hurt her child and she was seen as having done nothing about it. The abuser wouldn't necessarily be removed from his victim and the problem would be worked on with joint, family counselling. This has fallen out of favour, and now the blame is usually placed squarely on the shoulders of the perpetrator. He is removed from the vicinity of his victim. The children, it is now finally acknowledged, have the basic right of protection. The risk of it happening again is too high, and the consequences too great to have the perpetrator close by.

I was a fully grown woman before I could clearly see for myself where the blame truly belonged. The negative effects of my abuse reached their tentacles into every corner of my life. The guilt I felt took my freedom emotionally and physically; I couldn't break through an utter disconnect from my body and struggled with closeness in relationships.

It has never been easy for me to be emotionally at ease with men. My consensual, adult experience of sex has never been very relaxed, and I've often found it difficult to be emotionally present during it. Several times I have had sex without even minding whether I'm treated with sensitivity or care, and have been haunted by frightening flashbacks.

My relationship with my mother was complicated. Even though we were close in so many ways, I avoided talking to her about the abuse for so long – even longer than it took for me to discuss it with other people. I loved her dearly, and part of me longed to tell her everything – to cry in her arms and be a little girl again, being comforted and understood. Yet a barrier had been built between us when she found me in Grandpa's room as a child. A barrier that proved almost impossible to get past and I couldn't confide in her afterwards. The fact she might suspect something made me nervous around her and I was always so full of guilt and shame. Grandpa's ghost seem to loom over us constantly, and therefore I remained silent. Despite the fact that I lacked courage I made one honest attempt to bring up the subject in my adulthood, but I couldn't seem to find the right words and she didn't seem to have an idea of what I was trying to talk about.

In my mid-fifties I finally told her everything. I broke the vow of silence that I had made as a five year old when I stood on that stool in the kitchen all those years before. Well, I actually didn't tell her *everything* – I couldn't see the point of going into details. She was an old lady by then and I didn't want to upset her more than I needed to – but it was still very important to me that she knew the basics of what had happened to me in my childhood. It was a matter of survival for me, a matter of freedom, to break the silence that had reigned between us for way too long. I simply had to say to her what I couldn't say as a small child. So I told her that Grandpa had sexually abused me, but I spared her the horrendous details of the violence itself.

"That bloody devil," was my mother's response. She was someone who I had never heard swear before. This in itself was quite a reaction, and I somehow took this to mean that she had always believed, or at least hoped that the incident when she found me with Grandpa was an exception, not a pattern.

Even though I had now told her my Big Truth, the conversation didn't exactly flow afterwards between us. Neither of us could help the other to find the words, despite our mutual desire for closeness and understanding. My mother had to live with the fact that she had not been able to protect me. Her guilt was immeasurable, and however much I did not want to cause her pain, I could not protect her from this feeling either.

At the same time as my mother and I were having these strained conversations, official and public discussion around sexual violence was developing and becoming increasingly prominent in the media. My old ghost would appear if the matter ever came up when I was with my mother, and I would be back to not knowing what to do with my body, let alone my words. For a while it felt as if every time I went over to my mother's home (my father died in 2006) for dinner there would be something about child molestation on the radio or television, and I would become Ghost-beholden. After a very powerful TV programme that my mother and I watched together – in which a woman my age was interviewed about her experience of sexual violence in her childhood by a close member of her family – I managed to ignore my ghost. The programme enabled us to discuss the guilt that comes with being abused. Other than that, we were completely quiet on the subject until just a year or so before her death, when we finally had a good conversation about what had happened when I was a child. Mum spoke about the day she had come home early to find me in Grandpa's room. She told me how angry she was now with herself that she had not told my father about it. I want to believe that if he had known, he would have found a way to put an end to the violence. It was quite hard for me to find out that my father knew nothing at all about any of it. But in some ways, I had felt freer around him exactly because he didn't suspect anything. The fact I had lied to my mum was hard enough, as I spent so much energy as a child hiding the fact that my grandpa was constantly abusing me. My life was therefore partly a performance from an early age. I wasn't as stressed around my father because he wasn't suspicious of what was going on behind the curtains at Mörk. This made it easier to develop a relationship with him that felt relaxed and real.

The shame didn't go easily. It had staged a full and physical take-over of me, making me feel as if I didn't deserve to exist, to breathe and stand and *be*. It told countless lies *to* me, *about* me, on how worthless I was and how guilty. Belief in my own innocence was the hardest place to find, guilt was the only internal landscape I'd known.

Bluntly, how I see it is that my grandpa tore my heart out. He stole a very private and individual part of my *self*, and through this he gained total power over me, making it impossible for me to protest or confront him when I had finally gained an understanding of sexual abuse. And Grandpa sealed his crime with silence. His shadow became my shadow, and for years I spent all my energy trying to get away from his ghost. He changed his crime into a holy secret, the scripture being that the truth would send him to prison. Due to this secrecy, no one else knew the totality of me, and so therefore I perversely only felt whole when he was with me. For so many years he was the only one who knew everything about me, what I had experienced, and when I met him – the one who held a piece of my heart in his hand – I somehow felt complete around him. He was the only person who knew all my dirty secrets, my crimes and my shame. I would even say that as a young child I was filled with a strange sense of happiness when I saw him, as if it was a relief to be fully myself with someone. I experienced these feelings before I began to have an understanding that the wrong involved was actually a full moral injustice. I now know that this is a common consequence of this kind of abuse, but it was exceptionally difficult and confusing, trying to process and accept how and why I felt happiness around my abuser.

When I was four years old, and ill in bed, my Grandpa brought me the jar full of caramels. I felt so lucky and so fond of him. I was grateful for his kindness, which I took to mean that he was a good and generous man. Now I know this is another typical consequence of abuse. While there were times when I felt happy around him, there were also periods, especially later on, when all I felt was revulsion and shame. As a child, I was an innocent being who hadn't developed fully, emotionally or intellectually, and therefore I couldn't easily question what was done to me. My world was broken but I was unaware of it and didn't realise how stuck I was in an inhumane and unacceptable situation. Then, as I grew, critical thought grew alongside me. The rights and wrongs of society are learnt, and the learning in my case created massive self-judgement. Instead of seeing the abuse in its correct context, I continued to judge myself, and my child-self, well into adulthood. I kept this up until I was finally helped to see how defenceless the child is, how innocent. I was also told of how dangerous it can be to shoulder the blame for other people crimes.

What are considered in our society as 'normal boundaries' were crossed for me before I even learned to talk. This has resulted in my often having little understanding of where boundaries lie generally, and where to set them with people. My family jokes about me being a control freak – and there is some truth in this. I've had to learn to hold back and trust that other people can live their lives without my interference, and that I don't need to always be in control to keep everything from going wrong. The need for control is a normal response for someone who has experienced total loss of control, who has been powerless and dominated by others. You instinctively learn that it is better to be in control rather than being submissive.

Having a higher capacity for pain is another quite interesting result of my past. When I went to see a chiropractor, he couldn't understand how I managed to function with all the physical strain that stress was putting on my body. He said I should be writhing in pain on the floor due to the seriousness of my muscular rheumatism. I seem to be able to disconnect from my body, which results in me in hardly feeling any physical pain. My body can be swollen and infected, without me noticing it. I believe the body stores and remembers so many things that need to be released during the healing process of trauma, in order to fully recover.

One technique I would like to use more in my healing process involves looking at very specific, difficult memories and visualising them clearly; acknowledging them with the aim of releasing them and letting them go. We must not hide from our memories, but look at them kindly, facing the most uncomfortable ones and easing them into being acceptable to us right now. When we reach this point we can look back without terror and come to terms with the past.

My mother, although plagued with guilt, encouraged me to write my story and publish it. Her support filled me with strength. Some mothers would have preferred silence to shield the family from shame, but she knew I had to release my story in order to be free.

14

IN SPITE OF everything, I still wanted to live at Mörk throughout my childhood. I loved the downtown area, and the west side of Reykjavik was where I felt I belonged. I had many friends in my neighbourhood and it's where we played kiss and tell around the Rock in the garden in the evenings. However, staying there into my teens was not to be.

My family moved to Álftamýri when I was eleven. At the new place there was no ocean view, no oak tree reaching its branches up to my mother's kitchen window and our new home wasn't full of boisterous cousins. At Álftamýri there would be no beach with rocks to climb, no cafés – like my favourite, Hressó – where you could watch the strange characters of Downtown. There would also be no poets – like Þórbergur Þórðarson, who practised his Mullers exercises by the sea, splashing himself all over in the pursuit of health. I followed him once all the way from Ránargata to Grandi beach, where I watched him undress and start his exercises. I thought Álftamýri was terribly dull in comparison to the west side and far away from downtown Reykjavik.

One good thing about it was Grandpa stayed at Mörk with Begga and Júlli.

I missed my group of girlfriends very much after we moved, and would ride my bike over to visit them as much as I could. I stayed in touch with my friend Þórunn until we were about thirteen and she moved out of town to a village called Hafnarfjordur. It was around that time I started working at the fish processing plant in Grandi. Things were changing.

Just before her death, my mother told me she regretted moving to such a small flat. And the flat in Álftamýri was indeed tiny. My brothers shared a small room with just enough space for a single desk between two beds. I slept on a fold-out sofa bed in the sitting room, and the two youngest children (one who was actually born in the tiny flat) slept with my parents in their room. At the time, I never thought of our flat as crowded, but looking back on it now I understand what my mother meant about housing so many children in such a small space. My mother said she thought the conditions had not been good enough for us all, but I didn't notice, it was my home, a happy and safe place with my favourite people, and therefore plenty good enough.

My parents were never wealthy; sometimes they were not even solvent. Finance was a constant concern and we went through periods where my father's wages as a labourer fell short of covering the monthly expenses. When this happened, we would be forced to accept a short loan from either Aunt Fríða's husband, the dentist Stefán Finnbogason, or my father's old friend Hjálmar Torfason, who was a goldsmith. Both Stefán and Hjálmar were decent man and great friends of my father. Hjálmar's shop was on the main shopping street of Laugavegur, and I have happy memories of visiting him with my father. Around Christmas time my mother always received some of Hjálmar's beautiful hand-made jewellery as a present from my father. I liked Hjálmar so much that as a child I got it into my head that he was our cousin, and cried with bitter disappointment when I found out he was not.

My mother wanted her children to have advantages that her and my father simply could not afford. She would have loved for us to all have music lessons, to participate in more sports that included specialist training or equipment, and to be able to pursue any interest that came our way, without them being curtailed through lack of finance. I love her for her aspirations for us children and understand her frustration, which she expressed to me in later life, but I think we all did pretty well with pursuing our personal interests anyway. Joddi taught himself to play the guitar, going on to write songs and play in a band. Joddi and Sverrir played football – although I think their annual membership fees for the local club were sometimes overlooked by a kind manager when times were tight.

When my youngest sibling was about three, my mother wanted to go back to work – not least to ease the financial burden on my father. She trained as a postwoman, and took English courses at the downtown middle school, which she was told would help with her job. After her post office training, she started delivering mail, and later worked in the stamps office. Mum had also already taught herself to read and speak most of the Scandinavian languages – Danish being her strongest, due to all the Danish magazines Grandpa used to bring back to Mörk. Both Mum and Begga used to pore over magazines such as Hjemmet and Søndags BT, reading about the lives and loves of the Danish royal family.

In 1963, on the first day at my new school after the move to Álftamýri, I turned up with big braces on my teeth. My mum's brother-in-law, Stefán (Uncle Stebbi), the family's dentist, had given me the orthodontics for free. This was long before braces were common and the children at my new school considered them very strange.

Sometimes I think what prevented me from becoming ostracised or from being judged was that I was really good at sport, especially ball games. This made me popular in the playground, and very much aided my ability to make friends. However, I was not a particularly diligent student at Álftamýri. I had been very interested in maths, but I completely lost interest in middle school. It didn't help that my maths teacher was an older man who preferred to talk to us about the Icelandic Sagas than the subject he was paid to teach. He was an excellent storyteller though and this was my real introduction to what became a life-long love of the Sagas and Icelandic literature. Mathematically, all was not lost for me either, as after a couple of terms the maths teacher was replaced with a stricter teacher, and I caught up with the curriculum.

I went to high school at Hagaskóli on the west side and it was there that I started working harder. I eventually managed to graduate at the top of my year across all the schools in the country. There was even an announcement on the radio about it, and it felt like a huge victory for the poor kids who lived in public apartments in the same block of buildings as me; one of them had excelled and it made them proud.

I think the sense of achievement spurred me on. When I was sixteen I received an Outstanding Achievement award for German and Icelandic at my school. The prize was books; copies of Salka Valka, Independent People, World Light and The Fish Can Sing, all by Halldór Laxness. I recognised the author's name because my old friend Áslaug had first told me about him when I was just four years old. We'd been up in her family's cabin in Mosfellsdalur, and she'd pointed towards Gljúfrasteinn, saying:

"Guðbjörg, do you see that house?"

"You mean the one shaped like a B?" I answered (feeling very proud that I knew the letter B)

"Yes." Came the reply. "A famous person lives there. His name is Halldór Laxness and he's written loads of books." I remember feeling intrigued that someone famous lived 'just over there' and the name stuck with me. I learned over the years that he is read all over the world, and won the Nobel

Prize for Literature. Apparently, he had thanked his grandmother in his Nobel Prize acceptance speech because she had spent a lot of time with him in his childhood, and was a gifted storyteller herself. The first book I read was Salka Valka, moving on rapidly to World Light and then Independent People. I devoured them, and my literary love affair with the works of Halldór Laxness had begun.

In the year of 1967 I was confirmed in Neskirkja church, under the guidance of the Reverend Frank M. Halldórsson. Aunt Begga's oldest son was confirmed at the same time, so we shared a confirmation party in a banquet hall downtown. My mother's hairdresser friend put my hair up in a French twist and I had on a white dress, specially made for the occasion. Aunt Begga gave me a gift that I had a hard time accepting, and it wasn't for its financial value; it was my grandmother's wedding ring. It was solid gold, and for my confirmation Begga had asked for a deep blue gemstone to be set into it. Hjálmar Torfason did the setting, and it was done in a beautiful, modern design. What was most uncomfortable though was that the inside of the ring bore the inscription 'Jón of Mörk.' Begga put the ring on my finger and I had to wear it for the rest of the day. I'm sure she gave it to me because I had the same name as my grandma, but I found it deeply uncomfortable. It looked to me like a symbol meaning I was now Grandpa's wife. I had to hide the discomfort and smile bravely all day.

During my confirmation studies, I went through a period of thinking I might study theology one day and even go on to become a priest. I felt somewhere within me that God had given me the strength to withstand what I had suffered as a child and through religion I could transcend it, helping others who also suffered. In a strange way I felt that I had been specially protected, in spite of everything. I would sometimes feel a loving presence surround me and that feeling helped me create a distance from the pain. Perhaps I felt that conversing with God was my way of surviving –

escaping spiritually into a beautiful place that I recognized as Heaven. Perhaps it allowed me not to be emotionally present when horrendous things were taking place. I have read stories about similar reactions from others who have survived torment; for example stories of survivors of concentration camps in the Second World War. It reminds me of what I understand of Nelson Mandela's mental attitude when he was serving his prison sentence: there is a strength to be found in the certainty that you can control your own perspective and emotional state, no matter what the physical conditions and position you are in. Realising that your freedom of spirit cannot be taken away from you, whatever is done to you, is a way to experience freedom.

The psychiatrist and holocaust survivor Victor Frankl discussed this after his time in Nazi war camps. He discovered that human beings, with their unique ability to be self-aware, can decide within themselves the response to situations and the affect you allow them to have upon you. He found he could create freedom, when his body was being abused and had no liberty.

I'm not saying that violence comes without consequence. I was definitely bent and contorted under the abuse. But I had some kind of inner strength and joy that helped me survive and made it possible for me to go on to have an almost 'normal,' healthy life. Drug and alcohol abuse, mental illness and prostitution are all common results of childhood sexual abuse, all of which I'm grateful for having managed to avoid. Even though there are many things in my life that could have been less complicated I managed to create an independent life, full of love, happiness and a sense of humour. I have had a nurturing, very hands-on, human job which was rewarding to me and for all of this I'm grateful. I made a conscious decision quite early on not to feel sorry for myself for my experience in childhood, and pity from others has never interested me.

15

AFTER I HAD completed my teaching degree, I seriously considered studying theology. At the University of Iceland, the first woman to study theology had just been enrolled, although no woman had yet been ordained into the priesthood in Iceland. I felt this was unlikely to change in time for me to get a job, so I chose instead to study Icelandic Studies and then to go on and teach children.

Choosing to work with children was an important decision for me, and I hope that my experience as a child has given me strength to support children in many and varied situations.

I have always considered it to be exceptionally important to listen to and encourage children, as is, of course, keeping an eye out for any signs of trouble for a child beyond the confines of school. Being in a position to make a transformative impact on the life of a child has been incredibly fulfilling for me. Interestingly, it was my ambition to be the best school principal I could be, that gave me strength and finally turned me in the direction of getting professional psychological help for myself. A tragedy occurred when I was teaching at a college at Laugar in Reykjadalur in 1993. One of my students committed suicide, and the shock waves reverberated through the community. I consulted a psychiatrist in Akureyri for advice on how to support my students at this difficult time, as I hadn't been in this situation before. He emphasized to me the importance for those trying to provide support to also be supported themselves. He described to me how care-providers such as psychiatrists, psychologists and priests have their own people to talk their problems through with, not least in order to provide stronger support to their clients and parishioners. I realized I too could give better care by getting some kind of professional support for myself, having in mind my then undealt with trauma. In reality I was already looking out for a push to do what I had always known I should do regarding my own past. However, it still took me a while to build up to actually getting the help.

When I moved back to Reykjavik in 1996 to take over as Principal in Breiðagerðisskóli middle school, I started to look out for a therapist. In my research I found out that seeing a psychiatrist, rather than going to a psychologist, had the benefit of government healthcare subsidies.

A few years later, when I had become the chairman of the Reykjavik Principals Association, I tried to introduce to my colleagues the idea of all senior principals having a form of personal confidant for the workplace. The suggestion was not particularly well received and it seemed to produce mild incredulity that people in senior positions such as theirs may benefit from any kind of personal or psychological support, as if it revealed a weakness of some kind. Recently, I have noticed that this attitude is shifting. It is testament to the changing attitudes of the time towards mental health generally, that receiving psychological support to aid your performance in many careers and at a high level, is much more appreciated now and no longer an area for suspicion of weakness. I am happy that many principals have now chosen to look into it. Being a principal is a job that comes with much responsibility, and therefore the attached pressure and stress. Principals are bound by confidentiality in particular areas and are unable to talk about some inner issues at the school, and this is another reason to have a separate, safe space to express issues and talk through concerns.

———◦◦———

I can see quite clearly now how I've used my work to escape from my long-term pain. From early on I believe I developed a work addiction.   As a child, I was already quite entrepreneurial and earned myself a decent amount of pocket money. I don't think my parents knew how much money I had at my disposal. At first, my funds came from Grandpa, but this always felt uncomfortable. When I was quite young I started selling lottery tickets and various badges in support of the deaf. My friend Þórunn used to walk around the neighbourhood with me, knocking on doors. I learned every aspect of the neighbourhood from doing this job.   I learned names of the streets and pathways, the individual gardens; where there were cats and dogs; which of the people I saw around daily lived in which of the green and brown houses. I enjoyed exploring the different areas in the summer, the sun transforming the landscape over the long, long days; the light and shadows highlighting or casting aside the shapes of the corrugated roofs, as clouds streamed over the sky.

In addition to the door-to-door sales, I also had a paper round and babysat for children around the neighbourhood. One of my regular babysitting jobs was at Ránargata 46, directly opposite my house. Sometimes I'd invite Þórunn over, and we would smoke a few sneaky cigarettes after the children were in bed.   We'd been practising smoking cigarettes in a secluded local hut near Mörk since we were eight.

When I was thirteen, and again the following year, I worked for the summer months at the fish processing plant. I cleaned worms from carp from eight in the morning until five, seven or even eleven o'clock at night. It paid pretty well. The summer after, when I was fifteen and my mother was pregnant with my youngest brother, I changed summer job to the grocery shop in Viðir. When the shop closed at six, a kiosk opened there for the evening and I worked on into the night, serving drinks and snacks. The kiosk closed at eleven-thirty pm, when I would have to mop the floors before finally going home to bed. By the end of the summer I was exhausted, but my bank balance had significantly improved.

I started Hagaskóli High School that autumn, and found myself rather well off for a student. I continued working through the term time though, working as an assistant at Aunt Fríða's and Uncle Stebbi's dental practice in my spare time. I was always working, and looking back on it, too much so. I found it hard to relax, as if I was always running from something.

I finished High School in 1969, and immediately started studying for my degree at the Iceland College of Education, which later became part of the University of Iceland. It was initially my mother's idea for me to look into teaching, she felt it would guarantee me a job in the future. And I am grateful to the course not least because it reignited my passion for Icelandic literature, which I realise has been a constant source of comfort to me. Literature has helped me much in my life – allowing me to glimpse beauty amongst pages when I struggled to see it around me in the world. Many of us on the course were still in our late teens, and the youngest was just fifteen, so there was very much a college-feel to it. I threw myself into the social life, and was elected the President of the Student Union in my final year.

When I was there, the principal at the college, Broddi Jóhannesson, became worried about his students' alcohol consumption. So much so that he flew in a teacher from

Norway who advocated not drinking to teach us a lifestyle where we could have fun without alcohol. I'm not sure how much it affected the general student population, but his suggestion of gaining natural highs through being with nature and focusing deliberately on what lay around you, and being present, resonated with me. I still drank occasionally, but his ideas stayed with me.

True to my working form, I took the job of teaching very seriously from the start. When I was just eighteen I took on a full-time teaching job at Skógar Elementary, alongside working through my second year at college. Many of the girls around me were finding themselves boyfriends, and some were engaged by the time of graduation, but my focus was firmly elsewhere: on work. At Skógar I taught forty-three hours a week, which meant I had a fulltime job alongside my fulltime studies. I did not have any time, let alone desire, for sewing Christening gowns like some of my peers who were already planning for future family life.

I lived with the Principal, Jón Kristinsson, and his wife Maríanna Hallgrímsdóttir at Skógar, along with their three children. I liked my new environment; it was homely and seemingly far away from the still-looming shadow of Grandpa.

I liked my students from the beginning. Even though they weren't the most intellectual or sophisticated group, they were respectful and polite, despite my young age and inexperience. I found different, sometimes less academic, ways to reach them; telling them stories and creating short plays with them that would physically involve them. My favourite subject to teach was Icelandic. It gave me the chance to explore topics that intrigued me; people's feelings and experiences (both as an individual and within society), and how they are related and narrated in our literature and lives, and then how the literature circles back again to affect the feelings and experiences. I felt strongly about how literature and story-telling, in all its manifestations, can strengthen empathy in a person and in society.

It has been an ongoing interest of mine, looking at how literature can be used to develop individual emotional maturity and make sense of the world around us. I have always aimed to encourage my students to enlarge and strengthen their circles of empathy, and as Finch in To Kill a Mockingbird would say, you need to stand in someone else's shoes and walk around in them. The novels of Salka Valka for example, personally gave me the opportunity to view my own experiences through the prism of Salka's world. The novels of Halldór Laxness, meanwhile, have surreptitiously saved my soul more than once. Literature is a powerful tool in healing and attempting to make sense of this world we inhabit; I was passionate about sharing and exploring this with my students.

16

"YOUR GRANDPA IS DEAD."

Those were my mother's opening words when she called me at Skógar through the country telephone on February 27th, 1971. One short ring, one long ring. The country phone was an open line and I was keenly aware that other people might be listening.

"The funeral is on Tuesday," she said. "At the Cathedral." There was a long silence.

"Do I have to go?" I finally managed to get out, my body already shutting down; becoming heavy, as if weighted.

"What are you talking about?" she said. There was another length of silence, shorter this time.

"Of course you'll go to your grandpa's funeral." She said it quietly.

Over the last few months of his life, Grandpa had been a patient at the St Joseph's Hospital, and had repeatedly asked for me to visit him. I didn't go.

I didn't go, purely and simply, because I didn't want to see him. I could no longer even imagine the possibility of seeing him.

I know his last words to Aunt Begga were: "You were always so nice to everyone, weren't you?"

Other than this snippet, I know extremely little about his last days on this earth. I really didn't want to go to the funeral, but I went anyway out of duty. It would have been impossible to explain to people why I wasn't going, so I went. I was there at the church, and there at the graveyard.

Afterwards, I met up with some classmates from the College of Education, taking along my youngest brother Gylfi as a treat – and that's when I finally began to feel a sense of relief.

When Mum had called to tell me he was dead, an image of my grandpa had appeared in my mind – a cold, frozen, dead body. I felt neither joy nor sorrow in my heart; I felt nothing. No anger; no happiness. There was a void inside me, as if another ghost had turned up under the Eyjafjöll Mountains and sucked me dry of emotions and dry of my thoughts. I was numb, gagged and there was a lump in my throat as there often was when I thought about him, and what he had done to me.

In an attempt to escape the oppression of the ghost I went for a walk. I allowed the sheer beauty of my immediate environment to singularly hold my attention. I remained present by focusing deliberately on what lay around me. I noticed the blue sky, the birds flying high, a red truck driving by on Road One, with a brown trailer. I decided, as I had done before, not to feel sorry for myself and to live gratefully. Being alone in nature had yet again reminded me that the world is full of beauty.

When I moved to Skógar I had been offered my job at very short notice. I had little time to prepare and my wardrobe was especially meagre. I owned a good, sturdy pair of shoes and a thick woollen jersey knitted by my mother the previous autumn, but very little else to equip me for out of town teaching and living. My old neighbour at Mörk, Kristjana, who lived at Little-Farm, sewed a turquoise green 'school-teacher-dress' and a trouser suit for me. I loved them. I was grateful for everything life was now giving me, a great job within the Eyjafjöll Mountains that I felt held and embraced me.

Now that my grandpa was dead the scene had changed, as the villain was gone. For the first time I glimpsed the possibility of writing my story. However, I was still far from being ready to open up and it felt that society wasn't ready for the discussion.

The writer Marianne Williamson said once that it is our *light*, not our darkness, that most frightens us. I think about that often and how I've sometimes allowed myself to be blighted by a fear of my light – I have often feared to grasp golden opportunities and let my light shine.

When I visited Grandpa's grave, I stood there frozen. I was only eighteen years old and hoped to be free from the past, but I didn't realise how scarred I was. As well as blaming and judging myself I was yet to find out how my experience would affect my relationships with men; how sometimes, during intimate moments that should have been amongst the beautiful and liberating ones of my life, I would be confronted by flashbacks of the coal cellar. I had yet to understand how my body would never completely relax, no matter where I was or what I was doing. My shoulders were always hard and high, although I barely felt the tension.

I remember wondering during those days as a young adult if I'd always somehow be different; if I'd always be alone and never be able to have a normal family – never have a husband or children. I felt utterly inadequate for marriage, but somehow, despite (or maybe because of) my experiences as a child, I desperately wanted to have children. Children need so much love and security, and I felt I had a lot to give. I felt I could protect children from the dangers of the world and hoped that the day would come when a 'good man' would want me and we would have children. I wanted five.

I really enjoyed being with my students at Skógar that year. I was very pleased, and rather proud, that most of them had made significant progress in both reading and maths since my arrival. I felt strongly that it was my role in life to help young people, and I wanted more than anything to be of use to children in need – even if it meant moving to a foreign country and adopting street kids. I have never been able to cope with the fact that there are so many children in the world living with injustice. As I get older the desire to have an impact does not diminish. I still yearn to use my experience for good.

17

IN MARCH 1974, I went to see a play at the Reykjavik City Theatre.   It was called Candlelight, written by Jökull Jakobsson, and it had done well; it was mostly sold-out. It was an intimate play, and the atmosphere in the Iðnó theatre was cosy.   During the interval I went out for fresh air and stood by the lake, thinking about the play.   I was rather taken by the young male lead, who played the sensitive young boy, Kalli. His presence struck me as exceptionally warm and gentle, and I was captivated.

Not long after this, I went to a dance at the club Sigtún. In the crowd, I saw the young actor again, chatting with his friend. I felt I wanted to talk to him. Acting on my impulse I stepped across the room, interrupting with:

"Would anyone like to dance?" His friend declined, saying he wasn't much of a dancer, which left the actor.   He responded chivalrously and obliged by dancing with me. I loved to dance and we were soon in the centre of the floor.

Afterwards, I told him about seeing his play and I praised his performance, but he was soon chatting to other people. I felt slightly rejected, and returned to the friend I had arrived with. I told her about the actor and asked if she thought he was worth bothering about. She said he seemed interesting, but I realised nothing further would happen that night so I got on with enjoying the company of my own friends. We had some drinks, and danced.

A few days later I was out driving in my parents' white Volkswagen Beetle, when I found myself stopped at a red traffic light. I looked to my right and in the car next to me was the actor. I rolled down my window and we had a little chat. It was this exchange that became the real start of our friendship. After a couple of casual dates, and some long conversations about literature, I thought he wasn't interested in me romantically and was convinced that unfortunately this was as far as our relationship would go. Around this time, the actor had a breakthrough role in the musical Hair, and also wrote a hit song Dark Roses, so he was becoming well-known in Reykjavik. This made him especially popular with the female cohort of Iceland, but the actor himself found he was craving a serious relationship – and there, in front of him, was me, with my yearning for a family and children already firmly in place. Slowly, love grew between us, which later bore some fruit.

I had graduated as a teacher in 1973. Two years later, almost to the day, on the twelfth of July 1975, I stood on a large rock by the Öxarárfoss waterfall, as a gold engagement ring was slipped onto my finger. Another year later I was a married woman. I started talking about having children as soon as I was engaged, but my husband was not quite ready, so we decided to hold off for a while.

Our first son was born in 1978 when I was a student at The University of Iceland, finishing my Bachelor degree in Icelandic Literature. I planned to sit my final exam on May 24th. There were the City Council elections on May 27th and I ardently supported the socialist party, The People's Alliance. My son however had other plans for me and instead of sitting my exam and voting, I found myself being tested on giving birth. I was ecstatic, and also relieved to have had a boy. I felt, no doubt due to my experience, that it must be easier to protect a boy than a girl from the dangers of the world.

Within our marriage, my husband and I were very open about many things. We told each other our secrets, and I decided to share with him what I had never been able to discuss with anyone. He was the first person I told I had been sexually abused as a child.

He told me he wasn't willing to participate in any type of conspiracy of silence around my trauma and felt I should speak up about what I'd been through and share it openly with others. This shook me, as I wasn't ready to do so, and felt suddenly uncomfortable, even scared, that he could now potentially bring it up whenever he chose, to whomever he chose. This made me think I would have been better off not saying anything to him at all. I felt that the way sexual abuse was spoken about in society was still very judgemental and I disliked the thought of people having misconceptions about me because of what I'd been through. I felt that in the eyes of the community, survivors of sexual abuse were second-rate and damaged goods.

There were red flags early on in our relationship, even before we got married. The biggest one was his jealousy. I tried to ignore it, and deliberately focused on his good points – which after all were numerous. I found him immensely fun to be around, and he taught me a lot, for he was knowledgeable and well-read. We both loved literature. Despite of all this, problems were still arising. It felt as if he could be two very different men; one when he was in a good mood, another when he was in a bad mood. When he was feeling low or angry, the atmosphere in our house could be stifling and even when he was in a good mood, there was always nervous tension for it could change at any moment. Our backgrounds were different, however, we had both brought childhood dysfunction to our relationship. Our interactions confused me and I did not trust my own judgement or instincts when it came to knowing what was acceptable and healthy in a relationship. I would end up blaming myself and started to believe that everything that went wrong was my fault, that I simply wasn't capable of being in an intimate relationship.

Since my husband was so energetic and had so many different interests, there was never a dull moment with him. I liked being out and about with him, being immersed in a play, film or concert. He had an 8mm camera and would film everything we did. Because of this, there exist innumerable hours of footage of various family gatherings with relatives both alive and now long gone, as well as of our children in their developmental years. There are idyllic shots of us on our honeymoon in the Canary Islands; newlyweds running across the beach and eating juicy grapes in bed. We looked, and indeed were, deeply in love; for the good moments were as good as the bad moments were bad.

However, by the end of the honeymoon in 1976, I should have realised that our relationship was heading in an unhealthy direction. As much as we had walked arm in arm along the beach and run laughing into the ocean, there had also been lacerating fights and dreadful emotional turmoil. I returned as a new bride to Iceland, half-broken. But it was still early days, so I still hoped I could heal our relationship and work through the frightening arguments. I think I was blinded by my need to have children and create a family. As was now customary for me, I kept my problems – this time regarding my marriage – firmly to myself. I managed to convince myself that despite its fundamental weaknesses, I could make the marriage work.

Despite this underlying fault line in our relationship, we still managed to achieve many things together in partnership. We won the Reykjavík Scholastic Children's Literature Award for our translation of Jan Terlouw's novel Pjotr, ran a country school together, put on plays and made radio programmes. It seems to me now that we worked remarkably well together creatively and professionally. It was just as a private, intimate couple that we fell short.

One year we put on a production of Birgir Sigurðsson's play Pétur and Rúna. My husband directed, as well as playing Pétur; whilst I played the role of Rúna. At one point in the play, Rúna had an angry outburst and so as an actress I had to portray these uncontained feelings. I was in big trouble as my own feelings were inaccessible. The director however did not give up on me and he pressed me and pushed me until he found the trigger we were looking for. My character became engulfed in anger; I was swept away in a feeling I will never forget. I was very thankful for the experience. It was an extremely healthy catharsis, letting go completely on stage every night, as Rúna had her meltdown. My performance was very well received.

After our first child was born, I was occupied with family life. Most of all I wanted to build a house of our own and buy a car. I wanted to take out a huge loan to do so but my husband believed it impractical so we didn't. Later we regretted it as it turned out that the loan would have evaporated with the unpredictable inflation of the period. Instead we made do by fixing up an old basement in Skerjafjörður. It was there where we properly started our family life together.

My husband had other dreams than just raising a family. He wanted to study drama and we decided on London. First he went to London by himself, but I soon found myself a job as an au pair, and our son and I were close behind him. The job was with a wonderful Icelandic couple, married doctors, and the three of us were invited to live with them. Helgi Valdimarsson and Guðrún Agnarsdóttir had created a happy, cultured, artistic home for themselves, and we all enjoyed living there. To me, this was the happiest time of my marriage. I wrote countless letters to my mother back in Iceland, which I came across again only recently when sorting through my parents' estate with my siblings. On 6th March, 1979 I wrote:

Darling Mum,

We are doing well over here. Thank you for the card, I received it this morning. You can certainly say that spring has arrived in London. Last Sunday we all went for a family walk and your grandson was sitting up in his carriage without a hat or socks. We grown-ups only had our sweaters on, it was so sunny and mild. Today it's a bit windy so it's not as warm. A few bees have woken up already, and here and there you can see little blue and yellow flowers starting to bloom.

... Look at me just blathering on and forgetting to tell you the big news. Well, we kind of feel a bit naughty because... we decided to make another child immediately! And even without asking our parents beforehand. So there it is! The little one could even be here in time to be a birthday present for my mother in law as I'm due around the 18th of October. We couldn't be happier. The only thing that's causing us concern is the thought of you at home worrying about us. There is no need. We've spoken to our doctor-couple and they are very pleased and supportive – Guðrún is already figuring out the best place for a crib. I will probably give birth at St. Mary's hospital where Helgi works, they have a great maternity ward. Princess Anne gave birth there.

I'm still suffering from some morning sickness but luckily my husband didn't have class until 10:30 this morning so he brought me tea and biscuits to bed and fed our little guy while I took a bath. I'm so looking forward to your visit and I'm sure you are going to like it here...

The night our daughter was conceived there had been a lively discussion in the doctor's house about the appropriate period of time that should be left between having children. Helgi said that a year and a half was the perfect gap, since that meant the children could be good friends and play with each other. My husband and I therefore calculated on the spot that this theory meant that we needed to conceive on exactly that very night, in order for our kids to be born a year and a half apart. So, true to plan for once, exactly nine months later, on October 23rd 1979, our daughter was born. On October 29th the young father wrote this short message to his mother-in-law from London:

Hello everyone!
We have great news, the birth went well and we've enclosed a couple of photographs of our expressive and handsome daughter. Guðbjörg is healthy and doing well. After she was fully dilated, which took about six hours, she only had to push for about five minutes and the baby was born.
Send our love to everyone.

P.S. Big brother asks that granddad keeps snorting tobacco, so the little guy can keep doing his impression of him.

We moved back to Reykjavik in 1979, after two years in London. In 1981, when my daughter was two years old and my son was three, I filed for divorce. I think that sometimes, when two broken people meet, and even fall in love, the separate pain in their chests is magnified by the other until it is unendurable. This, I feel, was my husband and I. It takes just the right combination to cause the explosion, but we had that formula. I believe now that such a mixture, creating such a maelstrom of emotion, can be considered as a catalyst for good change and growth *through* the pain. It can be used as an opportunity to heal deep wounds. However, if an unhealthy pattern of communication is unavoidable, then it is vitally important that both parties get away. Then they can start their own individual healing, without the torturous influence of their partnership. Luckily for us, both my ex-husband and I were prepared to work on our individual issues albeit separately, and we have done a lot of work on ourselves since we split. It was a difficult marriage and a painful divorce but time did heal, even though I sometimes regretted what could have been.

During the divorce some of my old pain and tears finally loosened. My old ghost loomed over me again with new energy, especially after I heard that my newly divorced husband had told some people about the abuse I had suffered as a child. I didn't know who he had told, or how many people, and the unknowing, the uncertainty made me very anxious.

One evening, soon after my husband had moved out of our apartment and I was there alone I felt an overwhelming need to express myself. I decided to get my words out onto a tape recorder. I felt that there was no one in the world that could begin to understand me, it had to be that I was defective and I didn't trust anyone to listen.

That night when I recorded my voice I finally found freedom for the first time to speak out loud about my pain, my loneliness and my dirty secrets as honestly as I possibly could. Tears of an unfamiliar release streamed down my face. This was the first time I confronted my grandpa and real anger came. I howled at him like a dog and it felt healthy. It's a shame that shortly afterwards I destroyed it, ripping out the ribbon and smashing the plastic case. It was a testament of my journey – but it documented my pain and I couldn't risk someone coming across it and finding out my secret.

Three years after my divorce, I resigned as a teacher at Kvennaskólinn College when I was suddenly offered the position of Principal at Skógar Elementary School. It was a small school; I oversaw twenty-six students and there was just one other teacher – that I got to hire. I duly moved to Skógar with my children, where I feel they found a freedom you can only really find in nature. They put down strong roots in Skógar and were happy.

Soon after we moved to the countryside I went for a long walk by myself. I went up the mountain by the side of the waterfall and it felt like being reunited with an old friend. The spray tickled my face, and I felt cleansed.

In 1986, I took a one year sabbatical to finish a Master's degree at the University of Iceland. That's when the silence between my mother and me started to feel suffocating. In January I wrote a poem to her whilst sitting in the study hall in Árnagarður. It took me almost a whole year to find the courage to send it to her. Eventually, I wrote it in her Christmas card. I promised myself that I would one day be brave enough to look unflinchingly at my old memories, and even share them with others. I felt I needed to piece the fragments together that lay broken and scattered deeply within me, in order to finally be whole.

18

EVERY SUMMER I ride about on my green bicycle. I usually pass the Hallgrímskirkja church and head onwards to the west side. I like to watch the evening sun doing its fading dance over the sky, it feels nostalgic.

Tonight, I take my bike out on a different route. When I get to the west side I ride straight to the place where Mörk used to be. A light breeze moves across my face, as I pedal up Drafnarstígur and past the old kindergarten. Ever since Mörk was destroyed it saddens me to visit my old neighbourhood. It feels like the life that took place there has been erased as well. Cold concrete now replaces the smooth corrugated iron that was ripped down and thrown away. I do have a few photographs that my cousin Jonni took when the house was being demolished in 1985, and although they bring pain, I am grateful for them. Back then I wanted to find a way to preserve Mörk. In my opinion the old renovated houses of the west side are the most charming part of Reykjavík.

I get off my bike at Ránargata, and peer over a white fence, to where my old garden used to be. I hope I am left alone and nobody comes. I need to be there and the threat of interruption does not stop me lingering, for I need to find out if anything is lurking there. I have to know if there are any remnants of my past, so I can bring old memories back to life. Then something strikes me and a tear runs down my face. The Rock! It's still there. This is where I listened to my mother's stories; this is where we children played and picked flowers and made dandelion wreaths to put in our hair. The Rock appears to be the only thing left on the property from the past but as I start to leave I see the little white arrows on the path. They are not the arrows I made as a child of course, but they look as if they could be. It is a new building and there are new children but the same chalk game I played with my siblings continues.

And what happened to the old stone house that stood next to Mörk, the mother of the old stone house we called Little-Farm? And what happened to the coal cellar, and to the lorry that brought the coal and dropped it down, down into the Black Hole; the sooty chimney and the dirty smoke winding up to heaven? Where did it all go, and why didn't anyone want to preserve the old houses?

I am still very attached to my childhood home. Part of me wants everything to be exactly as it was; even the old futon in Grandpa's room, with the wooden wardrobe where his clothes hung, and the black and white picture of Mary holding the baby Jesus. I want to sit at the round kitchen table upstairs and look out over Ránargata, polishing my mother's silver. I want to wander on, into the living room and look out at the big oak tree above the Rock, where the birds nested. I want to wake up in the morning to the cooing of the pigeons that lived in the huts all over the west side of town. I want to watch them being fed from Grandpa's palm. In fact, I want the old houses to still be there, as living proof of everything that took place, of the people that lived at Mörk; so that nobody can say it didn't happen or the people didn't exist.

All my life I've wanted to spend my old-age in the house with the enchanted rock in the garden. Now when I stand here with my bike, staring at the Rock, I feel as if the presence of the new, concrete house built over the crumbled foundations of Mörk weighs down upon my childhood memories. The new basement is completely different from the coal cellar at Little-farm and it is the only place I am relieved to be rid of. I am relieved that the Black Hole with its darkness doesn't exist anymore.

———◦◦———

As I cycle home, the sky is on fire over the west side. The wind plays with my hair as I promise myself never again to be frightened of my memories. I choose instead to see the good in my past and feel gratitude to everything that has shaped me and led me to where I am now. Lines from Still Life with Woodpecker by Tom Robbins come to my mind; "It's never too late to have a happy childhood."

At Mörk, I met with shadow and light, it was where I spent a lot of time trying to figure everything out as I grew up. It was the life force of Mörk that kept my ghost at bay, holding down my silence that later would turn into an inner scream so loud I feared it would drive me mad.

When my daughter was studying Theology at the University she brought up the issue of child abuse in our society. She was concerned about the silence around the subject and felt that teachers might be able to help. At this I could no longer remain silent and simply told her what I had been through as a child. She had just turned twenty-three years old. Unfortunately, I didn't get to tell my son what had happened to me, he found out from another member of the family when he was just fourteen years old. It was a major shock for him.

My daughter was a baby, a toddler, a teenager, and I had not found the right time to tell her my story; nor had I known if it would be the right thing to do. I am glad to have taken the opportunity when it arose – even though I sometimes think my children could have avoided unnecessary emotional complications if they had not known about my past.

I had to live where there were shadow creatures lurking, but God knows that's not what I want to pass on to my children or have them carry for me. A large part of me would have preferred to have left a letter, for them to read when they were sixty years old. I admit there are times still when I wonder if my children's lives would have been lighter if they had never found out.

When I get home, I put away my bike and slip off my shoes and coat before going into the kitchen. On the wall hangs a photograph of Mörk. I am used to it being there, and normally barely notice it, but today I take it down and inspect it carefully. Life looks back at me, and also death. There was darkness in Mörk, and there was also life and light. Perhaps they cannot be separated: life is in death and death is in life. I thought of the Black Hole, and the smell of my mum's baking, the sunny kitchen window. It is all kept together, in the same drawer inside me. The photograph has accompanied me whenever I've moved, hanging on the wall wherever I've lived. Perhaps, though, I have only ever really lived in one place. I have never managed to move out of Mörk. Does that mean I still live in a house that was demolished years ago? It was a house so full of life, but death was there too, living in the dungeon and breathing hellfire.

The water is boiling in the kettle. I make some coffee and make a pancake, which I'll eat with blueberry jam and cream from the fridge. The pink shawl my mother crocheted for me is around my shoulders, and I curl up on the red velvet sofa in the sitting room. I eat the pancake slowly and look at the house in the photograph. The picture frame is made of old iron from a window frame, rusty like the corrugated iron of the house itself. When I lived at Mörk, it was already dilapidated, the gables were starting to crumble and it was beginning to fall apart. The house that had once been newly built had turned old.

Staring at the picture, the image blurs and merges with my memories. On the window sill there now sits a young girl, looking at the high chimney of Little-Farm and watching the coal truck come and go. A battered bin stands by the stone house in the same spot where the coals were dropped into the coal chute. My mother sits in the living room, an infant nursing at her breast. The baby girl suckles, then pulls away, seemingly transfixed by the leaking milk. She fastens herself on again. She looks at the breast and at her mother; there is wonderment in her eyes. Inside me, these pictures fade and redevelop. I let them.

I look at the photograph in front of me afresh, staring again until another image forms. My grandpa appears wearing his hat, in front of Little-Farm. The ghost stands beside him and he motions for me to come inside the coal cellar. I know I must obey – but for the very last time. He reaches his hand out to me, and I say a silent prayer as my feet find the steps. I make my way down the stone steps alone; breathing deeply and slowly. I descend one solitary step at a time. Neither Grandpa nor the ghost follows me; I am alone. I can feel a sense of peace washing over me. The trap door stays open and somehow everything looks different down there. I see my mother waiting for me with her arms open, and countless candles emblazon the whole cellar. I run to her, and allow myself to tell her all the things I've always wanted to say. On the wall hangs the picture of Mother Mary and her Child. I gaze at the picture on the wall, feeling the peace and security of a mother's love.

My mother carries me back up the stone stairs and into the light. The brightness of the sun shines through the doorway, and we pass through into it, closing the door behind us. The garden looks enchanted. We sit on the Rock and she strokes my hair, telling me a story about a princess who writes adventure stories. The stone farm and the timber house are gone, and the Rock is the only thing that remains.

Before I close my eyes, I see the ghost merging into my Grandpa and together they waft, as one, up to the heavens, as smoke from a stick of incense.

I put the photograph down and close my eyes, picturing my grandparents holding hands as they walk down a sunny road.

Falling asleep on the sofa, I dream of a beautiful butterfly with colourful wings. The sun lights up the sky as it flies through the old town of Reykjavik. The rays touch the butterfly's delicate wings, where the turquoise shines brightly; casting shadow on its dark body.

Acknowledgements

I want to thank my translators Áslaug Torfadóttir and Helen Priscilla Matthews for their generous work. Thanks to my English editor Tracey Scott-Townsend, also Philip Scott-Townsend, for believing that this story needs to be heard outside of Iceland. Wild Pressed Books is very much a publisher that feels right for my mother's story.

I would not have written this book if not for my mentor the author Vigdís Grímsdóttir, and to her I'm forever grateful for her encouragement, belief and support. My editor Guðrún Sigfúsdóttir at Forlagið in Iceland welcomed me when I sent her the first draft of the Icelandic version: Mörk, and both her and Vigdís served me with embracing support throughout this sensitive process.

Nobody has been more important to me in the pursuit of this project than the members of my family. I would like to thank my parents, whose love and support are with me in whatever I pursue and who both helped me when it came to writing the book. Thanks to authors Guðrún Eva Mínervudóttir, Þórunn Erlu- og Valdimarsdóttir and Þórdís Elva Þorvaldsdóttir for giving valid notes and support. I also wish to thank my loving and supportive partner, Sigurður Guðjónsson and my three wonderful sons, Flóki Hrafn, Árni Guðjón and Dagur Kári, who provide me with love and inspiration every day.

I know this story would not exist without the courage of my mother and her painful past. Therefore she gets my deepest thanks and respect.

About the Author

Thora Karitas Arnadottir studied drama in the UK and has worked as an actress for most of her life, appearing on stage, in films and on television. Thora is best known for the award winning TV series, Astridur, in her home country and for hosting Unique Iceland, a highly popular travel magazine show about Iceland.

And the Swans Began to Sing is the English translation of her creative nonfiction Mörk - saga mömmu (my mother's story), which was nominated for the Icelandic Women's Literary prize in 2016. Thora is currently working on her first novel, which will be released in Iceland in 2019.